The
Dance
Halls
of Spanish
Louisiana

The

Dance Halls

of Spanish
Louisiana

Sara Ann Harris

PELICAN PUBLISHING COMPANY
Gretna 2017

The word "Pelican" and the depiction of a pelican are trademarks of Pelican Publishing Company, Inc., and are registered in the U.S. Patent and Trademark Office.

ISBN: 9781455623334
Ebook ISBN: 9781455623341

Lower left front-jacket photograph: Edward "Dween" Nunez at De Pope Launch and Tavern on his 101st birthday. (Courtesy Edward Nunez, photograph by Sara Ann Harris)

Maps by Norris Designs

Printed in the United States of America
Published by Pelican Publishing Company, Inc.
1000 Burmaster Street, Gretna, Louisiana 70053

Contents

Acknowledgments

The Dance Halls of Spanish Louisiana is dedicated to Irvan Joseph "Pooka" Perez, past president of the Canary Island Descendants Association, who first introduced me to a kind and proud Spanish Louisiana community.

I want to acknowledge the Isleños for their generosity and graciousness. I am honored to have provided a forum for their story. I tip my hat to the talented singers, dancers, musicians, storytellers, cooks, gardeners, shrimpers, crabbers, and tradition bearers of the Isleño heritage.

A debt of gratitude is owed to members of the Los Isleños Heritage and Cultural Society who kept the fires burning after Hurricane Katrina, when prospects for the Isleño Revitalization were bleak.

Finally, I thank those fine individuals who welcomed me to their kitchen tables, onto their fishing boats, and to their local dancefloors and willingly told the stories of the legendary dance-hall days of Lower St. Bernard Parish.

The
Dance
Halls
of Spanish
Louisiana

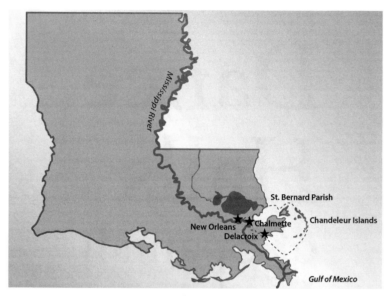

St. Bernard Parish is southeast of New Orleans. Founded in 1807, it was originally a rural parish where fruit, vegetable, sugarcane, and beef trades prevailed. Coastal Louisiana communities, including those in Lower St. Bernard Parish, conducted prized seafood and fur operations that in their peak years led their fields nationally and beyond.

Chapter 1

Vestiges of the Dance Halls

Thomas Gonzales walked into the nightclub like a man who had never doubted his place in the world. He and his six brothers grew up in Delacroix, a village about thirty-five miles down the road from New Orleans in southeast Louisiana. His first language was Spanish. He learned his trade (shrimping) from his father, his first and only boss. At seventeen years old, Thomas, like every other young man in the village, went into business for himself.

Thomas and Joan Gonzales walked past the long oak bar at Rockin Rumors, a popular nightclub in Chalmette, also southeast of New Orleans but much closer than Delacroix. It was Saturday night and they took their regular seats at a length of abutted card tables covered with red cotton tablecloths. The ceiling fans hung low from exposed beams and circulated cigarette smoke around the club.

The night started out slowly, as people were home watching a preseason New Orleans Saints' football game. Still, the first band began playing at 8:00 P.M. They sounded strong: a decisive drummer, a clean electric-guitar player, a relaxed bass man, and a couple of sassy horn players; all about the same age as the clientele, sixty and over. A second band would play from midnight until 4:00 in the morning.

When the band began playing "Brown-Eyed Girl," Thomas glanced toward the dancefloor, then gently touched Joan on the shoulder with the back of his hand. They got up in tandem. She followed him to the floor. Thomas reached behind him with both arms and Joan took his hands in hers, an entrance they had obviously used before. Then, he swung Joan out from behind him and the show began: two steps up, one step back, then two-stepping side by side, a spin—all in easy synchronicity. The familiarity between the two people was somehow both matter of fact and intimate.

All of the boys in Thomas's family learned to dance from their father. Thomas danced with his legs. Close friends called him "Spaghetti Legs." A man of small stature, Thomas stayed low to the ground and whipped his legs here and there unexpectedly. He moved like a cat, a weasel, a snake. All the while, Joan sang the words to "Brown-Eyed Girl" and stepped and swayed to Thomas's lead.

After their dance, the couple returned to the reserved row of tables, which was filling up. People with surnames such as Torres, Alphonso, Marrero, Ramos, Rodriguez, and Garcia—whose families had sailed over from the Spanish Canary Islands—sipped their beers and snacked on chips they'd brought from home. Almost all these people had grown up in Delacroix and other Spanish Louisiana villages in St. Bernard Parish, which borders New Orleans and extends southeast to the Gulf of Mexico. Thomas's older brother Richard "Kayo" Gonzales and his wife, Lillian, had also come out to the dance. In an earlier conversation about the dance party that Saturday night, Lillian had asked Kayo if he wanted to go. He said, "You know me. If there's dancing, I'm ready to go."

A woman wearing a shiny blue blouse walked toward us, arm in arm with a tall fellow sporting a cowboy hat. They were glowing. The couple went from person to person in our group and gave everyone a kiss. The word was he was her new boyfriend. Someone asked, "What is his name?" Someone else across the table said in a stage whisper, "It doesn't matter. She's going to kill him." I must have looked startled, because the same man chuckled and explained, "She's had three husbands and they all died." True to form, these people were always ready with a quip or a nudge.

Thomas and Joan Gonzales were well known for their fancy footwork at Chalmette dance clubs. (Courtesy Thomas and Joan Gonzales, photograph by Sara Ann Harris)

Allen "Boogie" Perez and Thomas Gonzales gathered with Spanish Louisianans and friends at Rockin Rumors nightclub in Chalmette for Saturday-night dances. The men were born in Delacroix, St. Bernard Parish, and danced at the legendary dance halls there when they were growing up. (Courtesy Allen "Boogie" Perez and Thomas Gonzales, photograph by Sara Ann Harris)

At St. Bernard Parish nightclubs today, folks gather on Saturday nights to share their passion for dancing and relive their memories of the legendary dance halls. (Courtesy Thomas Gonzales, photograph by Sara Ann Harris)

Couples gathered to dance at Chalmette clubs every Saturday night, a custom reminiscent of the dance-hall galas in the early twentieth century in Lower St. Bernard Parish. (Courtesy Doris "Dotty" Beaunos and Gerard Patterson, photograph by Sara Ann Harris)

Looking for a reading light, I pushed my chair back and walked over to a niche where a couple of pool tables stood, each lit by a hanging green globe. Some of the women were there looking at the *Times-Picayune*, the New Orleans newspaper, which had run a three-part cover story about Spanish Louisiana villages and coastal erosion. The readers were pointing to photographs of familiar faces. Their sense of togetherness as they delighted in the pictures from their past was palpable. Then, I looked over at the dancefloor. Twenty or so people in rows stepped from side to side. A petite, eighty-nine-year-old with an upswept hairdo walked out and joined the line dancers. Step for step, they all kept the beat. Like a flock of pelicans lilting across the sky, the dancers seemed to be elements of a single organism.

I went to the club that night to meet this group, because earlier I had visited with their parents, who told stories about *their* parents, builders of dance halls in the Spanish Louisiana villages of St. Bernard Parish. The more I learned about those dance halls, the better I understood why these couples were religious about getting together in Chalmette to dance every week. They had cut their teeth on what some anthropologists called the "Legendary Dance Halls of Spanish Louisiana" (1900-65).

The identity of those villagers, and to some extent that of these Chalmette dancers, can be understood in terms of character: their occupational character (for example, Thomas's pride in operating an independent family business), their social character (as related to cherishing their togetherness, like the women at the pool tables), and finally their individual or philosophical character (as exemplified by their understated sense of humor or the joke about the woman killing her boyfriend). On a deeper level, their humor was linked to an acceptance of life on life's terms. In the face of hardship, they dodged despair with lightheartedness. The underpinnings of this identity were cultural traditions, especially a passion for dancing, but also traditional Spanish Louisiana food preferences, the distillation of Old World spirits, speaking their native Spanish tongue, and singing *decimas* (Spanish Louisiana folksongs). They had tenaciously maintained their identity from the time they sailed to Louisiana from the Canary Islands (1778) until approximately 1900. But by the onset of the twentieth century, modernization of their lives and mechanization of their folk trades threatened to unravel this distinctive fabric woven of character and cultural traditions. Fortuitously, at that time the Spanish Louisianans built dance halls, where their identity was rejuvenated. However, the Dance Hall Era was their last hurrah.

As my evening with Thomas, Joan, and the other revelers drew to an end, they reluctantly closed out their reminiscences about the dance halls of Delacroix, St. Bernard Parish. Thomas said, "Oh, it was a whole other world down there on 'The Island'" (as they called Delacroix). Samuel Armistead, scholar of the Spanish ballad and friend of the Spanish Louisianans, seemed to concur. He described the community of the dance-hall days as "a variant Spanish world."

Chapter 2

Precursor of the Dance Halls, 1778-1900

Vestiges of the Spanish Louisiana identity still lingered at the Chalmette nightclub get-togethers, residuals of a vitality that swelled during the dance-hall days. The history of the people who built those dance halls answers questions about their Old World life, their cultivation of Spanish traditions, and then their adjustment to early life in Louisiana. Ultimately, it also informs their twentieth-century sense of identity that was rescued at the dance halls.

During the Age of Exploration, Spain pursued foreign lands in a grand way. Among the conquests were the Canary Islands (1400s), an archipelago south of the country and off of the coast of Africa. Spain dominated the lives of the Canary Islanders and employed many as field hands in what evolved into lucrative agricultural industries, such as sugarcane, orchil (lichen that yielded a violet dye), and wine. By royal decree, the Canary Islanders were registered as Spanish citizens, and their intermarriages with continental Spaniards who had relocated to the islands became commonplace. Conversion to Roman Catholicism was tantamount to a declaration of the islanders' loyalty to the mother country. Spanish Canary Islanders faithfully attended church services, which were followed by Spanish cultural activities on the church grounds. This integration of religious and cultural gatherings traveled with the islanders to Louisiana.

Spain accepted control of the Louisiana Territory in 1762 in order to build a protective buffer between the Spanish colonies on the Gulf of Mexico (Texas and Mexico) and England. The

Spanish were alarmed by the number of English military assigned to West Florida (then on the Louisiana border). King Carlos III of Spain authorized recruitment of Spanish Canary Islanders, and other colonists from exclusively Catholic locales, to build a Louisiana garrison. When England attacked Louisiana cities and other Gulf Coast sites, Col. Bernardo de Galvez countered with a well-organized militia, including a small representation of Spanish Canary Islanders. In the end, Spain successfully forced England off of the Gulf Coast entirely.

As part of the recruitment package, Spain had offered the Spanish Canary Islanders land grants. The contract also included passage to New Orleans under the spiritual guidance of a chaplain and the medical care of a surgeon. Spain was to build their homes and provide domestic animals; seeds for crops; farm tools such as hoes, shovels, and axes; needle cases, thimbles, yards of linen, and textiles; hats; stockings; handkerchiefs; food rations and medicine; plus gunpowder and a monthly stipend for one year, when the colonists were expected to achieve independence. When settlement in Louisiana proved to be grueling, Spain extended the stipend for four years. As family farmers, the Spanish Canary Islanders were expected to provide the citizens of New Orleans with much-needed food products.

The transport of Spanish Canary Islanders was the only en masse emigration of Spanish civilians to Louisiana. An estimated 2,200 men, women, children, and nursing infants disembarked on Louisiana soil between 1778 and 1783. By rule, all adults were under thirty-seven years of age. The men included individuals from Portugal, Seville, Galicia, Genoa, Asturias, and Valencia, who had relocated to the Spanish Canary Islands earlier and married island women. By comparison, the population of New Orleans was roughly 8,000, including French families, Spanish militia, Spanish public officials, Spanish merchants, free people of color, and slaves. The brave Gov. Bernardo de Galvez was at the helm.

Galvez directed the newcomers to settle at four locations that surrounded New Orleans. Clockwise beginning southeast of the city, they settled Pueblo de San Bernardo on Bayou Terre-aux-Boeufs (meaning "River in the Land of Buffalos," as designated earlier by the French), Barataria to the southwest on Bayou des Familles, Valenzuela (Brulee, then Donaldsonville) west of the city on Bayou Lafourche, and Galvez to the northwest on the Amite River.

When arriving at the Bayou Lafourche site, the islanders were said to have leapt from their transport and danced. This outburst must have soothed the anxiety that burdened these salt-of-the-earth people who had been at sea for three months and were many thousands of miles from home. As it turns out, their misgivings about the new place were justified.

The difficulties of living in south Louisiana cannot be overstated. Wrathful cyclone winds, destructive floods, and disease-bearing

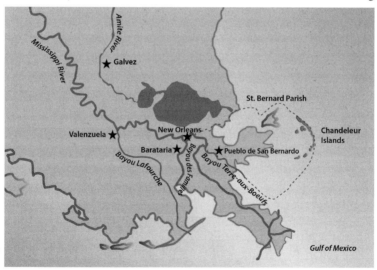

Anticipating British aggression, the Spanish Crown settled the Canary Islanders at four strategic locations in order to protect the port of New Orleans and Spain's international commerce.

insects resulted in crop failure, starvation, and illness. Within a few years, settlers of two of the villages had either died or relocated to the Bayou Terre-aux-Boeufs site. Gradually, those who settled on Bayou Lafourche largely assimilated with a nearby Acadian-French colony. Some families requested and were granted permission to relocate to New Orleans and Cuba. The Bayou Terre-aux-Boeufs settlement, then, was the only Louisiana village where Spanish religious and cultural traditions were to survive. At their early community gatherings, the Spanish Canary Islanders (now referred to as Spanish Louisianans) cultivated these with as much aplomb as circumstances allowed.

Bayou Terre-aux-Boeufs flowed from the Mississippi River southeast to the Gulf of Mexico (the west boundary of an area soon to be named St. Bernard Parish). Towering stands of cypress and tupelo trees and majestic bottomland hardwoods crowned the lowlands. However, a two-mile-wide band of high ground of an extraordinarily rich composition of soils straddled the bayou. Spain assigned land grants to the settlers within the band. With their agrarian background and Governor Galvez's support, the Spanish Louisianans managed independent family vegetable farms and fruit orchards. They hauled product by ox-drawn carts to the New Orleans French Market and sold to restaurant food purveyors, as well as fresh-food distributors that serviced grocery stores in the small city.

Two of the original ships from the islands had been delayed in Cuba, and a number of voyagers decided to make Cuba their destination. However, most of the group continued on to Louisiana in 1783. Many of this group were from the Canary Island of Gomera, where they had made their living fishing. They settled Benchijigua (later called Bencheque and then Reggio), also on Bayou Terre-aux-Boeufs but farther south than the first settlement. Oak forests dominated the area, but it was near a marshland of connecting bays and bayous that all held terrific promise for seafood harvesting.

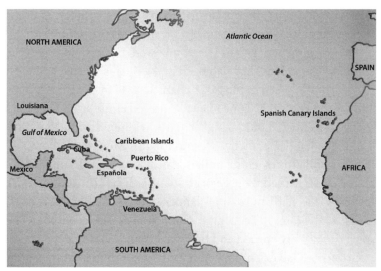

During the colonial era, Spanish Canary Islanders sailed to Louisiana and settled. They also emigrated to Texas (not shown), Mexico, Cuba, Española, Puerto Rico, Venezuela, Paraguay (not shown), and other Spanish colonies.

Roman Catholicism had been the foundation of life in the Spanish Canary Islands. Unfortunately, the only church in south Louisiana in 1778 was *Iglesia de San Luis* (St. Louis Church, which after a fire in the French Quarter was reconstructed and called St. Louis Cathedral). The French priests did their best to service Catholic settlers in the surrounding rural areas, traveling, weather permitting, by boat or horse and cart. It rained frequently and the roads were barely tracks in the mud.

At the Bayou Terre-aux-Boeufs settlements, the priest met villagers for holy mass at their homes or a designated common ground. He administered the precious sacraments (rituals that marked milestones in a Catholic's life). The Spanish Louisianans were especially concerned that their babies were baptized, their marriages blessed, and their deceased given the last rites. On his sporadic visits, the priest administered baptism to a group of babies at one time, then matrimony to several couples, and last rites to all those who had been buried since his previous visit.

The sacramental rituals were followed by festivities on the common ground, as they had been in the Spanish Canary Islands. All ages participated in the galas, characterized by the good humor and togetherness that came to be recognized as the signature social traits of Spanish Louisianans. It goes without saying that they spoke one language, their ancestral tongue. Musicians strummed familiar folk tunes and families danced in festive rural attire. Home cooks served their favorite Spanish dishes (including those featuring the native Canary Islanders' preference for vegetables, fruits, and grains). Then after the colonists sipped homemade spirits, jocularity ensued and they sang island folksongs.

Governor Galvez built his home near the original settlement. It wasn't long before the site was named *El Pueblo de San Bernardo* (St. Bernard Village), in honor of the governor and his patron saint. He visited the colonists on occasion and in all likelihood participated in the religious services, particularly the Feast Day of St. Bernard. He said he enjoyed the people's passion for dancing and their sense of humor. Their religious life was intrinsically linked with affirming cultural customs. As the heartbeat of their community, the get-togethers on the common ground were the precursors of the dance-hall gatherings.

Approximately a decade after the islanders settled on Bayou Terre-aux-Boeufs, Spain donated 200 acres of land to the Roman Catholic Church. *El Cemeterio de San Bernardo* (St. Bernard Cemetery) was built, followed by *La Iglesia Catholica de San Bernardo* (St. Bernard Catholic Church); a common ground was also set aside on the property. It was a dear moment in the settlers' religious and cultural life when a Spanish priest moved into the local rectory. Indeed, the core identity of the Spanish Louisianans, both religious and cultural, was strengthened by the presence of a Catholic church on Bayou Terre-aux-Boeufs.

A stained-glass rendering of St. Bernard, illustrating his devotion to the Blessed Virgin Mary, adorns St. Bernard Catholic Church today. His holiness was the patron saint of Bernardo de Galvez, governor of Spanish Colonial Louisiana and benefactor of the Spanish Canary Islanders. At St. Bernard Village and St. Bernard Church, Canary Islanders gathered for religious and cultural commemorations. These get-togethers were the precursors of the dance-hall galas. (Courtesy St. Bernard Catholic Church, photograph by Sara Ann Harris)

Catholic priests directed the religious observances at the church, including special feast days in honor of saints and virgins who were believed to be protectors of the parishioners. The Spanish Louisianans were primarily from two of the seven inhabitable Spanish Canary Islands, Tenerife and Gran Canaria. When oppressed by hardship, the faithful prayed to their patrons for intercession with God Almighty that He might be merciful. The immigrants from Tenerife sought the divine assistance of *Virgen de Candelaria* (Virgin of the Candles), and those from Gran Canaria prayed to *Virgen del Piño* (Virgin of the Pines).

The church pastor also planned activities on the common ground, where the colonists were swept up in their merrymaking, seemingly their social birthright. A journalist for the *Weekly Picayune,* a New Orleans newspaper distributed to rural sites, visited Pueblo de San Bernardo on a Sunday in 1838 and wrote: "They are of a very social disposition, delighting in each other's

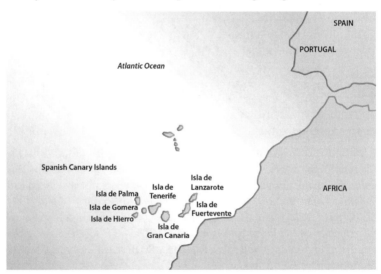

Spanish Canary Islanders emigrated to Louisiana in 1778 from the seven inhabited islands of a complex created by volcanic activity. There were smaller, uninhabited islands within the archipelago.

society . . . they possess a natural politeness, an easy, unaffected address."

He added, "The social virtues are warmly cherished. No one enjoys a pleasure unless his neighbor partakes with him . . . and thus are the best feelings of the human heart cultivated by the singular customs of this community."

In addition to social character, Spanish Canary Island music customs were gaily expressed on the St. Bernard Church common ground. To appreciate their colonial musical styles and folkdances, it's useful to visit present-day fiestas held in St. Bernard Parish. Spanish Louisianans commemorated their traditional character and customs at the fiestas with performances and exhibits.

Canary Islanders across the Atlantic were engaged in their own renewal. Often, they built events around feast-day commemorations. In some island villages, after mass on holy days, revelers joined their neighbors in playing Hispanic music, singing, skipping down the village streets, and dancing in colonial attire.

In 1991, St. Bernard Parish organizers began inviting Canary Island neighborhood musical clubs to perform at the Louisiana fiestas. These island visitors may have outdistanced colonial Spanish Louisiana villagers in terms of the diversity of musical styles and range of talent, but the authenticity of their performances was edifying.

La Parranda de Teror (Merrymakers from Teror) warmed up onstage at the 2010 fiesta in St. Bernard Village. Forty-six dark-eyed, dark-haired men strummed their instruments. They accompanied a chorus from the village of Teror on the island of Gran Canaria. The lead vocalists were assembled stage right and rehearsed among themselves. Then they turned their attention to the director. He began the performance dramatically with an *Isa* (the musical style suited for a fiesta).

The full sound of male voices lifted from the stage. The rich blend of the strings rose beneath it: mandolins, classic Spanish six-string guitars, *lauds* (lutes with six pairs of strings), and *timples* (the quintessential string instrument native to the Canary Islands). The beat of percussion instruments grounded the piece. The crowd was entranced.

As festivalgoers clapped to the music, *Los Cabuqueros de Arucas* (The Pride of a Stone Excavators' Village), a neighborhood dance group named for the village trade, skipped out onto the dance area. The women were dressed in brightly colored skirts and scarves and the men in slacks and vests. They stepped nimbly and whirled one another around. Dance partners smiled at each other, lost in the moment. It was a romp in the sunshine.

After their robust performance, I invited the dancers to talk with me. We reassembled at the Spanish Louisiana library on the fiesta grounds. We sat down at a broad hardwood table, and they began by clarifying that the music and dances presented that day were representative of colonial-era traditions. The dancers themselves were quick to explain that they were not professionals. It was important to them that they were understood as everyday townspeople, just as their predecessors in colonial times had been. They had first met at one of the feast-day parades; it was happenstance.

Louisa Suarez Viera was tall, dark, and outgoing. She explained that authentic 1778 gala attire started with the cloth, a weave of cotton and wool. Spanish Canary Islanders had woven cloth by hand. For special occasions, they created quality fabrics. They added ribbons, extra folds, and decorative buttons—anything to dress up the outfit.

The women wore many layers: *pantalota* (pantaloons), several slips, and a skirt. A blouse and vest were adorned with a modest wooden rosary. Louisa explained that while doing farm work, the women had worn the rosary on the inside of the blouse to protect it, but at feast-day galas they were proud to wear it in view. And always, they covered their heads with *pañuelos* (scarves).

Miguel Medina Santana spoke with as much agility as he danced. He said male dancers had worn *cachoros* (dark wool hats) and *chalecos* (vests). They wrapped *wajin* (sashes) around their waists, which hung down on one side. If the man was single, he hung the sash on the left; if married, on the right. Mischievously, some married men tried to get away with wearing the sash on the left, so they could dance with single women.

In colonial times, Spain had heavily influenced the music preferences of the Spanish Canary Islanders. For example, the music and choreography of the Isa evolved from the famous Spanish *Jota*. On the Canary Islands, the Isa was interpreted as a sweeter and more nostalgic style than the Jota. Furthermore, the Isa of one island was distinct in some respects from those of other islands. Thus, dancing attire was an important identifier of Isa dancers from one island or another.

On the same island, localized innovation also played into the mix. The people of the mountain region, farmlands, and beaches each danced the Isa slightly differently. Still, the Isa was always recognizable by its characteristic joy, striking visual display, and intense three-beat rhythm. Other Spanish Canary Island folkdances influenced by the Jota included the fun-loving mazurka, polka, and *Punto Cubano*. Additional Spanish music styles adapted on the islands were the Canarian fandango and folia, described as just plain silly. Spanish Louisianan musicians of colonial times played such musical styles on their personal string instruments, while their friends at the St. Bernard Church common ground danced the Isa and frolicked wearing clothing the village seamstresses had sewn.

Gatherings at the church common ground were the precursors of the Saturday-night get-togethers at the dance halls in that they were family events, character building, and community declarations of cultural tradition. However, at the dance halls, the music and dance styles had become Americanized. Still, in their homes, the Spanish Louisianans continued to play Hispanic string instruments or recordings and folk danced together. It was their passion for dancing, rather than the particular music style, that endured at the dance halls.

Approximately five years after construction of St. Bernard Catholic Church, Hispanic sugarcane planters along Bayou Terre-aux-Boeufs succeeded in refining granulated sugar. This was already a lucrative commodity in other parts of the world but a first in America. When a New Orleans planter commercialized the process, residents from the Northeast and Atlantic states rushed into St. Bernard Parish—and the rest of the South—eager to invest in the new cash crop. A number of Spanish Louisiana vegetable farmers got into the business, others sold their land grants and took jobs as field hands, and still others sold their land and struck out along Bayou Terre-aux-Boeufs some ten miles southeast close to the marshland of coastal Louisiana. People today are reticent to discuss any details of this relocation. It seems a cold wind divided the Spanish Louisianans of central and lower St. Bernard. And it chilled their relationship for decades. In Lower St. Bernard, Spanish Louisianans found a new sense of themselves and identified as Isleños ("Islanders," in reference to the Canary Islands).

Amid the forests and wetlands of Lower St. Bernard Parish, farming was not an option. Past Benchijigua, on the southernmost trail of Bayou Terre-aux-Boeufs, Isleños settled Woodlake and Delacroix. The marshland or grassland was replete with ducks and geese. The estuary, or nursery grounds for aquatic species, was thick with fish, crabs, oysters, shrimp, and turtles. The Isleños adapted to this environment and built lives based on a natural cycle: hunting waterfowl, rabbits, and alligators and harvesting aquatic creatures when each was seasonally available. It was a subsistence lifeway, i.e., they collected enough from the wild to feed their families and support a small trade with New Orleans. They also tended small kitchen vegetable gardens, chickens, pigs, and milk cows to sustain themselves. They supplemented their occupational lifeway with fur trapping and pelt sales. In a Jean Lafitte National Historical Park report, the Isleños were described as "masters of the marsh."

In what may have been another unpleasant parting of the ways, some of these same families later relocated to Bayou La Loutre ("The Otter River"), also in Lower St. Bernard, and settled the hamlets of Ycloskey, Chinche (Hopedale), and Shell Beach. When the shuffling and shifting settled, as Prof. Joseph Valsin Guillotte concluded, Delacroix was the most secluded of all the sites and proved to be the stronghold of the Isleño identity. It seems apropos, then, that in the early twentieth century, it was the Delacroix villagers who built the original dance halls.

There is a dearth of information on nineteenth-century Spanish Louisiana character (social, occupational, and philosophical) and

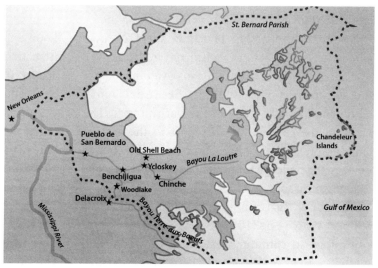

Of the four original Canary Island settlements (1778-79), Pueblo de San Bernardo proved to be the most successful. Many struggling Canary Islanders relocated to the more stable settlement. They founded six additional villages, one by one, in St. Bernard Parish.

cultural life (music and dance styles, folksongs, food, language, and spirits). Records of the fits and starts of church life in southeast Louisiana do, however, provide an indicator of Spanish Louisiana vitality, or lack thereof.

When the first pastor lived in the St. Bernard Church rectory in 1791, participation of the faithful was inspired and mass attendance grew. The Isleños in Lower St. Bernard continued to hold their Catholic faith dear; however, travel conditions, and perhaps personal squabbles, occasionally hampered their attendance at Sunday mass and the associated festivities. St. Bernard Church aspired to be a hearth to all of the Spanish Louisianans but, unfortunately, it wasn't long before the new rectory was vacant. Even though secular priests provided a degree of spiritual leadership, the gathering of loyal parishioners appears to have diminished. In fact, at that time, religious life in Louisiana became chaotic and referred to as the Dark Age. The rectory was empty for two additional five-year stretches.

Under the leadership of a few adept clergymen, Louisiana enjoyed a renewal of Catholicism, referred to as the Reconstruction of Faith. Bishop of New Orleans Antoine Blanc, the leader of the Reconstruction, visited St. Bernard Church in 1837 and commented on the piety of the parishioners. The next year, an entry in the church annual report to the archdiocese sang the church's praises: the interior for its ornaments and emblematic devices, the building for its handsome structure, and the landscape as being pleasant.

The church then came under the leadership of Fr. Jean Caretta for almost twenty years (1836-55). He was strong-spirited and wholly committed to community stability and structural improvement of the church. Father Caretta was respected for, among other programs, his work to expand services to the remote villages of the parish, including ministry to the congregations of Lower St. Bernard.

Fr. Antoine S. Doubter was recorded as also making a significant contribution, beginning in 1887, to a then-floundering St. Bernard Church. He executed fundamental changes to the physical structure of the church, which was described as ready to collapse, and breathed new life into the ministry. Like Father Caretta, Father Doubter was reported as traveling down the mud roads to minister to the Isleños in Lower St. Bernard Parish. According to church records, parishioners of Lower St. Bernard contributed alms to the church, however meager.

As it was difficult to transport the deceased upriver to St. Bernard Church, a cemetery was established near Delacroix. Then, in 1893, the archbishop of New Orleans arranged for the donation of a parcel of land for the construction of a church, school, and proper cemetery in Delacroix. Though the church was built, it was soon destroyed by a hurricane. It was reconstructed, donated to the Congregation of the St. Bernard Roman Catholic Church in 1896, and called St. James Chapel.

At the end of the nineteenth century, pastors of St. Bernard Church filed reports with the Archdiocese of New Orleans referring to financial difficulties and the need to raise funds. They held fairs and festivals for that purpose. Apparently, pastors in other parishes faced the same challenges, but not all church leaders were satisfied that festivals were the solution. Dissenters believed that these events were undignified and shamefully secular. Then, a 1916 papal decree was circulated to Catholic clergy in the United States objecting to their practice of hosting dinner dances.

The Most Holy Pope Benedict XV issued the decree and the archbishop of New Orleans distributed it to churches in the diocese, which included those in St. Bernard Parish. It read: for purposes of "procuring funds for pious work," of "becoming mutually acquainted," and of "strengthening the bonds of love and charity," the clergy has regularly invited Catholic families to "dances with feasting" and other amusements. The decree stated that this practice had gone on over the last 100 years and was to be "wholly abolished."

This pronouncement, along with the church records just cited, offer documentation that religious life and attending social activities hosted by Catholic churches were functioning during the nineteenth century in St. Bernard Parish. However, these records did not necessarily characterize its cultural life at the turn of the twentieth century as Spanish.

Other sources did indeed address the endurance of the Spanish Louisiana cultural life. Accordingly, throughout the nineteenth century and early twentieth century, culture was reinforced by the immigration of additional Canary Islanders as well as Spanish nationals from Seville, Galicia, Catalonia, Santander, and Andalusia. Also, Cubans, Puerto Ricans, and Mexicans relocated to the lower parish. Cultural discrepancies existed among these peoples, of course, but over time they assimilated in a manner that strengthened the Isleño identity.

Elders spoke fondly of small gatherings in each other's homes. They talked about getting together in the evenings to play string instruments, enjoy Hispanic folkdances, share Isleño dinners, speak Spanish, sing folksongs, and drink homemade spirits. Felice Lopez Melerine graciously agreed to an interview about a family gathering at her home. I knocked on the screen door of a modest house in central St. Bernard Parish. Felice answered, her grey hair brushed back and clasped in a comb. Inside, it was fairly close quarters. At her suggestion, I made myself comfortable at a small wooden table. The confidence in her carriage, even as she stepped slowly across the room, belied her ninety-two years.

"When I was about seven or eight, they had Spanish men down at Delacroix Island that came from Spain," Felice said. "My daddy was from Spain. And my uncle and them was fishermen, and they would go out and fish with my uncle and that.

"And my grandfather—his name was Tolero Gonzales—he had

a little gramophone, and he had the records . . . ," she continued. "You had to wind it because at that time, you didn't have no electric. And the Spanish men, the ones that knew how to dance, they'd dance their Spanish dances. . . . And that's how I started dancing. . . . They was wonderful dancers. . . . And that's how I started."

During the nineteenth century, gatherings at the common grounds, Catholic churches, and private homes nurtured the Isleño stock—both their cultural traditions and character. Socially, they were known for their affability and jocularity, but they could also be rowdy and even divisive. They clearly valued a togetherness that included all ages. Their work character was defined by a family occupational unit. And work in the wetlands taught them community reciprocity, i.e., their survival demanded interdependence. In terms of a philosophical character, the Isleños were realists; they gained peace of mind by yielding to life on life's terms. They adapted to forces more powerful than themselves: to nature's cycle of bounty and mayhem.

Chapter 3

Dance Halls and the Fur Trade, 1900-65

It seems that the fur trade was forever destined to dispense good fortune to the Louisiana marsh dwellers. Beginning with the colonization of North America, France and England competed aggressively over the fur trade in Canada and the upper Mississippi River Valley. They shipped pelts from America's East Coast to the Old World, where fashionable garments were produced and sold to the powerful and wealthy.

René Robert Cavelier, Sieur de La Salle, was a respected French explorer and fur trapper. He claimed the entire Mississippi River Valley for France (1682). When France later settled the port of New Orleans, they gained control of commerce in the whole of the nation's heartland.

Likewise, this presented France with the opportunity to ship pelts from the upper river south to their own docks. The city developed into a significant international fur-shipping center. Fur trapping in the lower Mississippi River Delta itself was then recognized as worthwhile. Louisiana marsh dwellers began trapping and selling to buyers, who then shipped pelts to England and Germany, the fur processing and distribution capitals of the world. Garments were sold in eastern and western Europe to an exclusive clientele.

At the turn of the twentieth century, Louisiana fur trapping, hunting, shrimping, crabbing, oystering, and fishing had all developed into relatively profitable mom-and-pop businesses, a steep step up from a subsistence economy. Isleños operated within a commercial network across southeast Louisiana that sold fur pelts, alligator hides, "dressed" waterfowl (cleaned and prepped for sale), and fresh seafood to the New Orleans market.

The Louisiana fur trade surpassed almost all of the other natural-resource occupations. Mink, otter, beaver, fox, raccoon, rabbit, and skunk had always been plentiful in the state. Bobcat and bear roamed the forests and were hunted for hides, though less frequently. When muskrat (a previously unnoticed furbearer) emerged, the state rose to the top fur producer in the country.

The fur trade improved the standard of living of south Louisiana communities exponentially. Wetlanders, including the St. Bernard Parish Isleños, built bigger, better wooden homes and boats. They acquired horses, automobiles, and trucks. And they installed gasoline-powered engines in their boats, converting them from sail power for the first time. The marsh dwellers bought consumer goods that made life more comfortable, such as iceboxes, fans, radios, and record players.

While the Isleños welcomed progress and modern conveniences, these lifestyle changes were displacing their family traditions. For example, with mechanization, fishermen and shrimpers worked farther from home and eventually stayed out on the water overnight. This change disrupted daily suppers, when family closeness reinforced their native culture. The Isleño association with their homeland was eroding. Gradually, Americanization was prying the Isleños away from a life centered around the Catholic Church, Spanish Louisiana food, language, singing and dancing, and spirits. Progress was both a blessing and a disadvantage. Fortunately, when they grabbed the brass ring, the Isleño fur trappers applied their winnings to the construction of dance halls—dance halls that were to steady the teetering Isleño identity, both their cultural traditions and their character.

The dance-hall experience, for example, fortified the work character, in this case that of the Isleño fur trappers. To appreciate the association between dance halls and the Isleño work character, it's important to understand the Isleño perspective on their occupation. Unlike a researcher attempting to understand Isleño identity, the Isleño did not compartmentalize it into cultural traditions, work character, social character, and philosophical character. Isleños did not regard their trade as a distinct sector of their lives or even separate from their core selves. Working in the marsh—shrimping or trapping—"is not what we do," Allen "Boogie" Perez, a Delacroix elder, once said. "It's who we are." And so, when Isleños walked into dance halls, they walked in as the whole of themselves. They were as much Spanish Louisiana folksingers as they were hardworking trappers. Consequently, the camaraderie at the halls strengthened their work ethic.

The Isleño work character was defined by a well-functioning family occupational unit. Fur trappers made camp in the deep marsh for the three-month winter trapping season. Every family member had a job, even the youngsters. And the expectation for them to deliver was unquestioned. As the cold crept into Lower St. Bernard, men and boys sharpened tools such as scrapers and knives and repaired traps. Women and girls packed supplies: family quilts (two to three inches thick), kitchenware, and dry goods. Males sailed or motored out some ten miles from their villages and built or refurbished two-room raised cabins. They dug cradles in the ground where they docked their pirogues (shallow-water wooden workboats).

In the evenings, the male set the traps along "runs" (frequently used muskrat trails). In the mornings, after a breakfast of ingredients gathered from the wild, the trapper set out for a day of trudging through wet grass, a canvas sack strapped on his back. He checked traps, removed animals, carefully skinned them, and stowed the pelts in his sack. He buried the meat in the marsh. Then, back at camp, the women and children cleaned or "dressed" the pelts, pulled them over wood stretchers, and set them in the sun to dry. As a family unit, Isleños were intelligent in the ways of the wild, resourceful, and collaborative. Dancing, singing, and dining together on Saturday nights sustained these strengths.

At this time, family fur trappers primarily tracked muskrat. The muskrat is an aquatic herbivore from the subfamily Arvicolinae, which includes voles and lemmings. It has a large, compact body and a tricolored coat and was named for muscone, a secretion used in the perfume industry. So ubiquitous was the muskrat in the marsh, and so defining was the trade to the Isleño identity, that a sign at the dance-hall entrance might have read Muskrat Lodge.

The furbearer's emergence in the Louisiana marsh was an ecological fluke. Before they trapped muskrats, Louisiana coastal families had hunted alligators. When European demand for alligator hides increased, Louisiana overharvested the reptile and its population dropped. Louisiana hunters at that time used marsh burning to flush the gators out into the open. Soon, the state prohibited alligator hunting and introduced an alligator conservation program that is still in effect today.

Muskrats naturally propagated very quickly. But when alligators, the muskrats' most voracious predators, were temporarily diminished, the muskrat population surged. Also, marsh burning caused a terrific growback of three-cornered grass, the mainstay of the muskrat diet. As these dominoes fell, the muskrat reached epidemic proportions across the Louisiana coast. Cattle ranchers were outraged by their destructive grazing, and rice farmers saw levees, which they'd built to facilitate irrigation systems, tunneled until they collapsed. Even fur trappers were initially disappointed when they found muskrats in their traps, as they were anticipating mink or otter. After several efforts to control the animal, the state opened and monitored a muskrat trapping season. Then as the national fur trade developed, muskrats unexpectedly weighed in as the champion of the Louisiana trappers.

Even more important to Louisiana's dramatic fur success was the global reinvention of the fur industry and the creation of new markets in North America. The chaos leading up to World War I

Due to ecological changes in the Louisiana marsh in the early twentieth century, there was a fur-animal epidemic. The state then set a regulated fur-trapping season. Isleño trapping families applied their new gains toward building the dance halls. (Photograph by Sara Ann Harris)

interrupted Europe's customary shipments of pelts. As foreign fur processors and garment manufacturers were forced out of business, the Modern Age of Fur (1910-60) rose in the United States. New fur-processing facilities in New York and St. Louis created the first domestic retail fur industry ever in North America. Surprising as it may be, the unassuming, clever, dance-loving Isleños, as well as the other Louisiana trappers, played a star role in this new theater. Furthermore, the dance-hall experience served as the behind-the-scenes director, as it were, that inspired the trappers/actors.

The new paradigm heightened the demand for North American pelts. Savvy advertising and the budding film industry brought fur fashions to the attention of entitled American men and women. The demand was intensified by a new niche market. During the war,

American housewives were employed as factory workers, welders, and machinists. They lost interest in the slenderizing long dresses and corsets of prewar days. They began wearing more comfortable dresses with fuller cuts and shorter hemlines. And their new outfits were accessorized with fur collars, cuffs, and hems. The elegance and style of fur became accessible, for the first time in the world, to everyone. Whereas the upscale American customer paid $1,200 for a sable coat, the working woman bought a trendsetting rabbit, squirrel, or muskrat jacket for $150. Louisiana was the primary source for these reasonably priced pelts that fueled the new market.

The national trade name for muskrat was "imitator," because frequently it was used as a substitute for more expensive furs. If ermine or mink were not available, a national furrier readily used processed muskrat. Also, to improve sales of Louisiana muskrat attire, leading marketing agents sold it under a fictitious name, such as "Hudson seal" and "Southern mink." Muskrat pelts were always in demand and Louisiana produced an unrivaled quantity of raw pelts. During its peak years, the Louisiana harvest, according to the Louisiana Department of Wildlife and Fisheries, far exceeded the combined take of Alaska and Canada. And in those years, on average, 80 percent of Louisiana pelts were muskrat.

Fur trappers and dance halls were linked by a local transaction. The halls were multifunctional. As the only large buildings in the villages, dance halls were gathering places, of course, but Isleños also used them as fur business centers.

Approximately every two weeks, trappers paddled their catches from the camps to the village dance halls. They sorted pelts and worked with buyers to set prices. But negotiations did not always go smoothly.

As the sale of Louisiana furs became more profitable, New Orleans businessmen dealt themselves into the prosperity. Some entrepreneurs who had once owned land tracts in St. Bernard, but had allowed property taxes to lapse and the land to revert to the state, persuaded the government to award them those titles again. In other cases, the state sold contested land to the highest bidder. Isleños found No Trespassing signs on the fur-trapping grounds. Families had worked in these wetlands for over a century, with no need to prescribe property as personal. The very concept of private property galled the Isleños. They perceived the business claims as outright assaults on Isleño honor and independence. The new landowners required rent from the trappers, plus a percentage of their fur profits. In response, some Isleños continued to trap on the so-called private property. The land grabbers then rubbed salt in the wound by hiring and housing trappers from Texas on Louisiana land. In the dance halls on fur-trading days, heated exchanges escalated into brawls. In the marsh, there was gunfire and the outsiders' cabins were burned to the ground.

Federal and state governments made arrests, and the disagreements were taken to court more than once. In the end, the court allowed two options to the Isleños: lease from land managers or the state, or buy their own tracts of land. As a measure of remediation, the American Farm Bureau Federation got involved. It was a newly formed national nonprofit organization that advocated for rural families. It had affiliates in every agricultural state in the country. Ordinarily the federation worked with small farmers, but they extended their services to Louisiana fur trappers during this conflict. Bureau agents made it their business to work at the dance halls themselves. They supervised the grading of pelts and posted guidelines for the setting of prices. They also assisted Isleños with applications for government loans for the purchase of property.

The dance halls were centers of conflict resolution between traditionalists and opportunists, each clamoring for their share of the booming fur industry. Unfortunately, solutions negotiated at the halls were not cure-alls. Injustices, financial and otherwise, persisted.

Chapter 4

The Dance-Hall Experience, 1900-65

Marie Louise, or "Weeshe," was a member of one of the largest Isleño families in St. Bernard Parish. She was a no-nonsense kind of gal who spoke her mind. I met her at the sheriff's office in Lower St. Bernard, her place of work. Weeshe's grandfather, Ernest Melerine, had once owned a dance hall in Delacroix. It was passed on to her mother and father. Growing up, Weeshe spent a great deal of time at her family's place. "Those were the good times," she said. "Family upon family having fun together. A few got rowdy, but most had a lot of fun."

The halls were large, open, utilitarian structures. Local carpenters constructed them using the "board-and-batten" technique, which accommodated the expansion and contraction caused by a wet climate. They used wide cypress boards as siding and covered the gaps between the boards with narrow strips of wood (battens). Builders also constructed "galleries" (porches) on the front and rear of the hall, where the crowd spilled out on hot nights.

I asked Weeshe to describe her family's dance hall. She picked up a pencil, drew it on a napkin, then walked me through it room by room. The long building was a "shotgun," a series of rooms arranged one after another. If someone had fired a shotgun on the front porch, the shot would have traveled clear through the doorways of the house and out the back door, hence the name. The first room of the dance hall was the bar. There, men ordered drinks, played cards, shot pool, and even gambled when the fur trade and whiskey smuggling were lucrative and everyone had spare change. Next was a large dance floor. Isleños spent hours there, whirling and laughing and staving off the troubles of an unpredictable and dangerous life in the wetlands. When they were weary and overburdened by personal losses, meager seafood catches, or destructive tidal surges, joining together at the halls was their solace. At the rear of the dance floor was a wide stage where a guest band performed. The children danced in a roped-off area next to the stage. Past the stage was a kitchen with tables and chairs. And attached to the kitchen was an alcove with cots where parents put their youngsters down at a certain hour. One parent always stayed to watch over the sleeping babies.

In addition to Ernest Melerine, Vincente Fabre, Arthur Molero, and Anthony Molero owned similar gathering places in the small village of Delacroix. During peak fur-trapping years, 250 people lived there. In Ycloskey, another village in Lower St. Bernard, Vita Molero and Mrs. Martin built halls. And on Saturday nights, the Isleños also reveled at Teta's in Reggio. Over time, others built halls in the central part of the parish.

The dance halls in Delacroix, it seems, had the best reputation. As the story goes, when young men from Delacroix went up the road to dances in other communities, the women there always asked them to dance first, as they were considered the best dancers. One Isleño said that was what started the fistfights every Saturday night—that and the infamous Isleño temper.

In Delacroix, the dances rotated from hall to hall. If everyone went to Vincente Fabre's place on the first Saturday of the month, then on the second Saturday they danced at Anthony Molero's, and so on. The reveling began at 8:00 P.M. and went on until dawn, some said. Infants, youngsters, teenagers, adults, elders—everyone attended the dances. Weeshe and other Isleños talked about the sense of togetherness at the halls, and it seemed to be what they missed most about those Saturday nights. It's safe to say that this close bond had been one of the defining qualities of the Isleño social character, ever since they first settled St. Bernard Parish. In the twentieth century, it was the dance-hall experience that helped perpetuate the Isleño value for community.

On Saturday afternoons in Lower St. Bernard, one of the dance-hall owners would drive to New Orleans and contract a talented black band for the night. As he drove the musicians back through the parish, they played from the bed of the pickup truck as an invitation to everyone. People flocked to the dance. Some rode horses; if they had a truck, they drove; others walked and caught rides with drivers along the way. Roads in St. Bernard were not paved at that time. Edward "Dween" Nunez, a lanky, white-haired man with a gentle voice and mischievous smile, told of going to the dances even after a hard rain.

"Yeah, I had a car then," he recalled with a chuckle. (He was laughing because he didn't drive anymore. He affectionately called his daughter his chauffeur.) "And the road was so bad we used to get stuck. They never had no 'shell' [oyster-shell surface] and no 'pave' [pavement], no nothing, gravel or nothing. We used to get stuck." So, he and his buddies would take off their shoes and start pushing the car. It would go that way on and off for seven miles. When they got to the hall, they would simply rinse off their feet and slip back into their shoes. It seems nothing could deter Isleños from attending social gatherings. Dween's story was an example of classic Isleño good humor. He and his pals considered the mud and the trouble of getting to the dances as incidental and probably joked about it later. Like many Isleños, Dween expected obstacles along the way, both simple and dramatic.

He continued, "It used to cost. . . . They used to put a badge on you, so they know that you paid. That was fifty cents . . . all night!" Dween chuckled to himself again, remembering how far fifty cents would go when he was a teenager in 1924.

Before Hurricane Katrina, Dween had evacuated from Lower St. Bernard to the safety of the central parish. Afterward, he took up Saturday-night dancing at De Pope Launch and Tavern, something he had gotten away from in his forties. Dween talked the band into playing a waltz, his favorite musical style from the dance-hall days. The night I interviewed him, he was celebrating his 101st birthday. As he wore his traditional Canary Island vest, danced the waltz, and smiled for pictures with one lady after another, it didn't seem that Americanization, drudgery, or hurricane winds had robbed him of his charismatic Isleño character.

Felice Nunez said that on Saturday nights, she walked down the road in Delacroix with other young girls: "I was twelve years old. I would love to go to the dances. I used to put [on] a little skirt and blouse, bobbysocks, loafers. And I would dance with them children" (her neighbors). She smiled as she told the story.

Edward "Dween" Nunez moved upriver from Lower St. Bernard to Violet to avoid the destruction of tropical storms. There, he harkened back to his days as a young man and danced the waltz every Saturday night. (Courtesy Edward "Dween" Nunez, photograph by Sara Ann Harris)

The halls held dance contests. "They would put tags on our backs," Felice explained. "And we would dance with our partner. They had two old mans that I loved to dance with. They used to dance the waltz. . . . One was a little old man. They came from Spain. And them two old mans, they dance so nice. I used to love to dance with them." The judges also marked the bottoms of the dancers' shoes at the heels with chalk. Good dancers were light on their feet and did not let the bottoms of their heels touch the floor. As the band played, the judges observed; they asked couples to sit down, one by one. When the music stopped, the couple who was still on the dance floor—with chalk intact on their heels—was the winner.

Often, Felice went home with prizes: boxes of chocolates, jewelry, dolls, American flags, and other memorabilia. She saved them for

The original Cocoanut Island Dance Hall was built in Toca in 1919. It did not escape the perils of coastal weather. This replica was constructed at the St. Bernard Village Isleño center after Hurricane Katrina (2005). (Courtesy Donna Mumfrey Martin, photograph by Sara Ann Harris)

years. And after she had children, she pulled her winnings off the closet shelf to show them and talked about the dance halls.

The Isleño social character, work character, and passion for dancing seemed to be burning bright at the dance halls. As noted earlier, Hispanics from various countries had emigrated to Lower St. Bernard Parish and assimilated with the Isleños. Local musicians still played traditional music styles for dancing at private homes, but it's not clear if this Hispanic music heritage found its way to the dance halls. At the halls, the Isleño affinity for Hispanic music and dances was morphing into an Americanized pleasure.

Most Isleños remembered dancing to jazz bands, rhythm and blues ensembles, and other talented New Orleans black musical groups. They told stories about dancing the jitterbug, polka, and waltz. Early jazz was characterized by rounds of improvisations by horn players. The genre grew out of the blues and a Southern Baptist singing tradition. According to accomplished New Orleans musician Wynton Marsalis, to appreciate the music one has to listen to what each musician personally communicates with his instrument. Jazz is a conversation among musicians. In the 1920s, Edward "Kid" Ory, a New Orleans trombone player, wrote what became a jazz standard. A lively tune and easy to remember, it was a variation of "The Old Cow Died and the Old Man Cried." Kid's music career had taken him to Chicago, where he recorded with Louis Armstrong. As the story goes, at one recording session they were short a song, and Kid suggested adding his yet unnamed tune to the LP. The sheet music had been stuffed in his briefcase for some years. Kid played it and Armstrong liked it. They did some arranging and then laid it down. Armstrong was credited for the song, titled "Muskrat Ramble." On Saturday nights in Lower St. Bernard, the tune must have put extra snap in any muskrat trapper's step.

Jazz musician Oscar "Papa" Celestin was born in Louisiana in 1884. He played guitar and trombone and performed in small towns early in his life. By age twenty, he was playing the cornet in New Orleans and, shortly afterward, started what became the wildly popular and enduring Original Tuxedo Jazz Orchestra. Greats such as "Bebe" Ridgley, Peter Bocage, and Louis Armstrong played with the group. The orchestra was hired out for both black and white society functions.

In interviews about dance-hall musicians, the Isleños raved about Papa Celestin. He performed in St. Bernard with a small traveling band. Their stories about Papa always turned to his rendition of "Lil' Liza Jane." The song dates back to at least the 1910s and became a standard both with and without lyrics. Many groups performed and recorded it in various musical forms: traditional jazz, folk, bluegrass, and rock and roll. Even New Orleans brass bands perform their interpretations of the song.

The dance-hall story about Papa Celestin went something like this. As the evening began to wind down, he played "Lil' Liza Jane." It was a signal that the night revelry was coming to a close. But this just could not be. So someone passed a hat and the crowd collected enough to hear the song again. And yet that still was not enough for the dancers. At this point, the storytellers were laughing and saying that no one wanted to go home. So they passed the hat again. "As long as we kept paying him, he would keep playing," one person said. "We danced to 'Lil' Liza Jane' for hours . . . until dawn."

The band was onstage so long that Papa Celestin started making up verses. He looked out into the crowd for cues and improvised with something like this: "Well, that sweet lady is dancing so good; but if she keeps on going, she's gonna lose her shoe."

And then the crowd sang the refrain: "Oh, Liza, Lil' Liza Jane; oh, Liza, Lil' Liza Jane."

Papa would sing, "Oh yes ma'am, yes ma'am, that is quite a dress. There's no other way to say it; you have been blessed." The crowd would come in with the chorus, and Papa would follow: "Well, if you just keep dancing, you will never feel blue. I might have to come down and dance with you."

And on it went.

Inez Campo was in Ernest Melerine's family, so she frequented his dance hall. Today, she lives across Lake Pontchartrain north of New Orleans, safe from tidal surges. I interviewed her by phone. "Papa Celestin made a lasting impression on me," she said. "In fact, I was really impressed with the way these guys could make people happy. Well, every now and then, a certain song comes my way—and it takes me right back to Uncle Ernest's hall on one of those Saturday nights."

When it came to rhythm and blues, New Orleans' own Antoine Dominique "Fats" Domino shook the rafters at the Isleño dance halls. No doubt, his rolling piano and distinctive vocalizing styles wowed everyone. Felice said, "They had a good time. The old people who didn't know how to dance [R&B], they'd go watch the young people. And they would bring their daughters and all that."

"It was really nice," Weeshe said. "Husbands and wives danced with their children in their arms."

Lillian Robin Gonzales laughed as she said, "My daddy loved to dance. He started the evening with my mom, but she got tired and stopped. He had to have three dance partners to get him through the night!"

In the summers, they must have danced until they had to stop under the weight of the humidity. Then perhaps they stepped out onto the gallery and cooled off. From the sound of it, when they strolled back in, they danced some more.

Traditional Dance Halls of Lower St. Bernard Parish

Bayou Terre-aux-Boeufs
Delacroix: Ernest Melerine's, Vincente Fabre's, Arthur Molero's, and Tony Molero's
Reggio: Teta's

Bayou La Loutre
Ycloskey: Vita Molero's and Mrs. Martin's

Isleños lived a modest life, even during the dance-hall days. Besides no paved roads and no electricity, there was no plumbing. Every home had an outhouse and a cistern for water. Ice was scarce, so a drink from the bar was tepid. Yet, in these moments on Saturday nights, the Isleños did not want for anything. They were exactly where they wanted to be.

Jeanette Perez Alphonso said, "Dad taught us to value simple things. Nothing money could buy was as important as what family could bring. It's not what you own or how much you have that makes life."

Irvan Joseph "Pooka" Perez, her dad, concurred. "You made a living. That's all you were looking for. Nobody was gonna be millionaires. . . . I was never sad. Those were the best days of my life."

Weeshe commented, "I do think that because of all the people we got to meet, when my dad and mom were in business [as dance-hall owners] helped us learn what life was all about."

Isleño jocularity and rowdiness were unleashed at the dance halls. Their sense of community and appreciation for family and hard work were also affirmed. And though they may not have continued their Hispanic dance tradition there, their passion for dancing clearly had persevered. Saturday nights also stoked a flame under other cultural traditions, such as feasting, speaking Spanish, folk singing, and drinking Old World spirits.

Chapter 5

Midnight Feast at the Dance Hall, 1900-65

At midnight at "The End of the World," as Isleños referred to Delacroix, everyone strolled back to the dance hall's kitchen. Some owners prepared and served meals; others hosted potlucks. A smiling grandfather may have ladled up steaming vegetable stew called *caldo* and shrimp cooked in rich Creole tomato sauce. Or a teenager might have helped herself to a serving of *chayote rellena* (mirliton stuffed with shrimp) and *alcachofas con salsa verde* (artichokes with green sauce). A youngster probably pointed and asked his mother for paella. Then one can imagine that a shrimper helped himself to a slice of baked wild duck and spooned up a dollop of crab and squash casserole.

Afterward, no one was shy about going back for dessert: *flan* (egg custard), *arroz con leche* (rice pudding), or *buñuelos de platanos* (banana fritters). The Isleño renderings of fresh vegetables and rice, plus Louisiana seafood and wildlife, left diners in pleasing dispositions and blanketed them with a sense of wellbeing. Like their other cultural experiences at the dance hall, the midnight feast grounded the community in its distinctive identity. After the meal, chances are people pushed back from the dinner table and took a few moments to relax. They may have strolled out onto the back gallery and sipped a liquor.

Dween Nunez sparkled when he talked about dinners at the dance halls. "Yeah, those ladies . . . I tell you, them people from Delacroix Island, they could cook well. Oh, it was good. Fifty cents! You get a whole bowl of gumbo. Seafood gumbo!" In addition to being popular, seafood gumbo illustrated the cross-cultural influences of Isleño fare. The stew started with a *roux* (a French, slow-cooked butter sauce). Okra or *file* (powdered sassafras), each a thickening agent, was simmered in the base until the desired consistency was achieved. Seafood, a decidedly Louisiana addition to Spanish Canary Island food, was finally stirred in and simmered. It was served over rice as the main course. Native Americans had first cultivated rice in the Mississippi River Valley and it became a staple in Louisiana cooking. An examination of the source of gumbo suggests other influences. Some researchers believed that the word "gumbo" derived from *guingambo* (Angolan for okra and the name of an African communal pot). Others suggested that "gumbo" was formulated from *kombo*, the Choctaw word for powdered sassafras.

Most dear to Isleño cooks may have been the ingredients originally gathered from Spain's far-flung colonies. For example, Isleños cooked with serrano peppers from the east coast of Spain, cayenne peppers from South America, and chayote (or mirliton, a vegetable native to Central America). Isleño cooks also inherited the Spanish Canary Island preference for vegetables. Early family farmers in St. Bernard Parish grew asparagus, artichokes, olives, corn, kidney beans, squash, potatoes, okra, bell peppers, and pumpkins. Isleño meals also featured *moles* (Spanish Canary Island cooking sauces). These signature blends of hot peppers, vine-ripened green peppers, olive oil, parsley, and other herbs enhanced the timbre of many an Isleño meal.

Louise Bonomo Perez grew up in an Italian community not far from the Isleños that had an impressive cooking tradition of its own. She married Irvan "Pooka" Perez as a teenager, moved to Delacroix, and learned to cook Isleño vegetable dishes from her mother-in-law and grandmother-in-law. It was a fine night at the dance hall when Louise served her caldo. Maida Owens, director of the Louisiana Folklife Program, wrote: "Mrs. Perez is especially well known for her caldo, a thick, nourishing soup traditional to the Isleños. . . .

The soup begins with white beans. Pickled pork and vegetables like corn, red potatoes, sweet potatoes, carrots, and sometimes squash are added later in the cooking process. . . . The caldo takes about two hours to prepare. Before it is served, the whole vegetables are taken out of the broth and arranged on a platter to be added to the soup as it is eaten."

Cinda Melerine prepared *papas arrugadas* (wrinkled potatoes), another Isleño favorite. She boiled small potatoes in their jackets in salted water over a low flame. When the potatoes were tender, she baked them in a covered dish until the skins wrinkled. Cinda served the dish with a choice of *mojo picon verde* (green dipping sauce made from vegetables) and *mojo colorado* (spicy red sauce).

The Isleño midnight feast was organic in that virtually everyone at the table had contributed to the preparation using ingredients cultivated in their own gardens, gathered from their yards, or wrested from the wild. And the art of traditional food production was not lost on the home cooks. They had spent a day or days selecting, chopping, or marinating ingredients until achieving the desired blends; they then parboiled, stewed, or roasted the dishes using time-honored techniques.

On the Louisiana coast, seafood and wildlife are plentiful, and Isleños embraced the bounty. However, to appreciate the significance of staging a feast, of successfully putting food on the table, it's important to understand the challenges of the fishing-hunting life. Temperature, rainfall, wind activity, water salinity, the nutrient load of coastal waters, cycles of the moon, and ocean tides all affect the production of abundant, high-quality seafood and wildlife.

However, from year to year these elements fluctuated. And so, as generous as the coastal wetlands were, they were also niggardly. Feeding a family on the Louisiana coast was always a gamble. Some fishermen called it a life of "feast or famine."

In good years, when natural forces aligned, Isleños harvested clusters of moist Eastern oysters, swaths of Gulf of Mexico shrimp, and tangles of fat blue crabs. They also graced the dance-hall dinner table with more than enough speckled trout and red drum (saltwater fish), diamond-backed terrapin (turtles), swamp rabbits, white-tailed deer, and mallards and pintails (migratory ducks). Pooka talked about the abundance. "The ducks would come in November most of the time," he said. "They were in the thousands. Oh! Lots of ducks." When the Isleños heard ducks honking overhead, they didn't look up to watch them fly by for a few minutes; they saw them flying over en masse for days at a time.

However, there were years of unproductive natural conditions and meager harvests, and then the Isleño community was vulnerable to hunger, sickness, poverty, and weather-related work accidents that took lives. Families suffered. The fishing and hunting life required coping with food shortages and personal loss. The Isleños learned to rely heavily on one another. Community reciprocity was another fundamental tenet of the Isleño work character, and compliance was taught to the young.

One afternoon, I met Pooka in the kitchen of a refurbished home that had been donated to the Isleños as a cultural center. As he sat at the table, he let his thick, tanned hands drop comfortably to his lap. I pulled up a light wooden chair, the seat worn smooth, and sat down. Even when talking about dire circumstances, the eighty-two-year-old spoke calmly.

"Down on the Island [Delacroix] was total isolation. Your boat was tied to the front of the house. I can remember I counted the boats. There were thirty-one boats. That was thirty-one families. Your boat was your most important possession." His father's boat was the *Seagull* and his grandfather's boat the *Early Buck*, a reference to a full-grown male deer grazing before dawn's light.

Everyone knew that they had to apply themselves to get food on the table, particularly in lean years. "You are on your own," Pooka explained. "It's up to you to do what you need to do. . . . You hustle

Neda Jurisic tonged for oysters on the family farm in Plaquemines Parish, which borders St. Bernard Parish. Home cooks in southeast Louisiana took great pride in serving oyster, shrimp, and crab dishes to their families and at special events like the Saturday-night dances. (Courtesy Eva Jurisic Vujnovic)

and you do what you got to do. . . . If a fisherman went out fishing [and] caught fish, he wouldn't sell any [in New Orleans] 'til the people from that little community had enough to eat."

He added, "It was our job, as a kid, when we came from school." Then he interrupted himself and quoted his father: "Take this bucket of shrimp . . . and take them to your aunt."

Pooka continued, "Or to whoever had lost maybe their husband and had small kids. We'd do that."

Pooka described his daddy as "lord and master" when he quoted him again: "Boy, when you come from school today, you take that ax and you go to your aunt and chop wood."

Pooka explained, "Chop wood for her, so she'd have wood for the winter; so they wouldn't have no misery, you know. This is one thing the old people had. Regardless of how hard they worked, they always took time to teach you what you should do. Especially a boy and, of course, the ladies would teach the girls."

Felice Nunez also told stories about community members working with one another. Isleños were fishermen and hunters, but they also tended "kitchen gardens" and small barnyard animals. "Everybody was poor," Felice said. "We would help each other. My husband's grandfather, he had beautiful [vegetable] gardens." And he shared produce with neighbors.

"Between my daddy and my mama, they started raising chickens," Felice added. "We used to pick baskets of eggs to give to the neighbors. We used to kill and clean the roosters. You couldn't keep the roosters because if you had too many roosters, the chickens wouldn't lay.

"We would give out baskets of eggs and roosters. And then they [the neighbors] would come and bring baskets of vegetables. That's how we did. We helped each other out there. It was nice when I was coming up, I'll tell you.

"Mrs. Robin had cows. A gallon of milk was ten cents a gallon. Fresh milk!"

During colonial times, family vegetable and fruit farms in the Deep Delta sustained local villages as well as the city of New Orleans. Families continued planting small "kitchen gardens" in Lower St. Bernard's dance-hall days. (The Historic New Orleans Collection, Accession No. 1974.25.13.53)

There was no doubt in anyone's mind that survival rocked precariously in the cradle of interdependence. Villagers stood ready to work with one another. The midnight feast at the dance hall was a glowing affirmation of their survival in the marsh.

The midnight feast—indeed, all of the cultural pleasures that the Isleños shared at the dance halls—fortified them in the face of hardship. But there was a level of chaos and destruction peculiar to coastal life that was indescribably more intense than the seasonal vagaries that determined Isleño food harvest. The natural phenomena in their wetland home greatly influenced the distillation of the Isleño identity. During the fall hurricane season, torrential rains and massive tidal surges, coupled with winds of 100 miles per hour or more, demolished communities. Coastal residents lost family members and friends to drowning and flying debris; their boats, homes, churches, trucks, bridges, and seafood docks were crushed.

From 1893 through 1965, eight Gulf of Mexico tropical storms and hurricanes made landfall near the mouth of the Mississippi River and traveled east, impacting St. Bernard Parish. Two of these were particularly ferocious. As they chewed through the landscape, the hurricanes shredded villages in their paths. The "Cheniere Caminada hurricane" made landfall at Barataria Bay in 1893. Devastating winds of 130 miles per hour and a ruthless tidal surge left 2,000 people dead. In 1915, an unnamed storm, twisting at the same brutal wind speed, crashed onto Grand Isle and plowed through every town in its path, killing 275 people.

The National Hurricane Center rates hurricane intensity by sustained wind speed. They use a five-category wind scale: Category 1, 74-95 mph; Category 2, 96-110 mph; Category 3, 111-30 mph; Category 4, 131-55; Category 5, above 155 mph. The two most intense storms to make landfall during the Dance Hall Era were both Category 3.

Natural catastrophe bred resilience in the St. Bernard Parish people. Isleños adapted by surrendering to the unfathomable forces. It was not resignation, in the sense that they felt downtrodden; it was humility, meaning they realistically acknowledged their position in the scheme of things. They achieved a sense of wellbeing that came from accepting life on life's terms. This might be called their psychological or philosophical character. The Isleños grieved their losses, returned, and rebuilt. However, after every storm, some families did move to upper St. Bernard, other parishes, and even out of Louisiana.

Unfortunately, there was another natural killer in the delta. St. Bernard Parish was very close to the mouth of the Mississippi River. The river's monumental basin was fed by nearly 40 percent of the nation's rivers. Melting ice engorged the Mississippi every spring. Historically, the river jumped its banks annually and flooded hardwood bottomlands along its run down to the Gulf of Mexico. For the protection of life and property, the United States

Hurricane Name, Date	Locale of Landfall	MPH Winds, Category	Deaths
Cheniere Caminada, 1893	Barataria Bay, just west of Mississippi River	130 mph, Category 3	2,000
Number 4, 1901	Grand Isle, just west of river	90 mph, Category 1	10
Unnamed, 1904	Mississippi River delta	130 mph, Category 3	0
Unnamed, 1906	Louisiana/ Mississippi	Small storm	350
Unnamed, 1915	Grand Isle, just west of river	Unrecorded	275
Unnamed, 1947	New Orleans	130 mph, Category 3	Unrecorded
Flossy, 1956	Grand Isle, just west of river	80 mph, Category 1	8
Betsy, 1965	Grand Isle, just west of river	125 mph, Category 3	Unrecorded

government built a levee system that eventually ran almost the full length of the river. However, the levees were not always able to contain the spring floods.

The country's most disastrous flood churned through the nation's heartland in 1927, causing mayhem along the way. At its most southerly point, the deluge of water hurtled through Louisiana and finally pummeled St. Bernard Parish. The depth and breadth of destruction in the parish was staggering. Families lost every tinder of their belongings. They saw loved ones swept away by the muddy surge. Furbearing animals, the center of Isleño occupational life, were wiped out. It took years for the citizens to recover. The Louisiana Department of Wildlife and Fisheries restocked the marsh with muskrat to support the fur trade.

Tragically, the flood in St. Bernard Parish had been exacerbated

Like so many rural families in the heartland of the nation and in the delta of the Mississippi River, the Isleños were pummeled by the Great Flood of 1927. A standing dance hall in Lower St. Bernard Parish provided a light at the end of the tunnel. (Courtesy Grun-Retif Photographers, photograph by William Henry Grun)

by human intervention. By dynamiting a section of levee, state government officials and New Orleans businessmen had rerouted the churning waters to protect New Orleans. The city was saved. Unfortunately, the levee break directed the flood, in all of its ferocity, into St. Bernard Parish. The strategic move decimated any trust the Isleños may have had in outsiders.

Historically, the Isleños had been ever mindful of the threat of raging winds and surging waters. The awareness grew into what could be called a collective psyche. If the dance hall was a hearth to the Isleño identity, and a healing center after Isleños were weakened by seasonal misfortune, it was also a light at the end of the tunnel following catastrophe.

In 2011, a visiting Spanish Canary Island band performed from the same folk-music tradition sung by Spanish Louisianans at the same location, St. Bernard Village. (Courtesy Donna Mumfrey Martin, photograph by Sara Ann Harris)

At the 2010 heritage fiesta, La Parranda de Teror, *a group of forty-six male musicians and vocalists, performed renditions of classic Spanish string compositions. The diminutive* timple *is a member of the guitar family and unique to the Canary Islands. It accommodates fast, rhythmic strumming.* (Courtesy *La Parranda de Teror,* photograph by Sara Ann Harris)

Canary Islanders visiting in 2010 danced to an Isa (a traditional form of music) in St. Bernard Village at the heritage fiesta. They prided themselves on performing to music of colonial times and dressing in attire of that era—just as their counterparts, Louisiana Spanish settlers, would have. (Courtesy *Los Cabuqueros de Arucas*, photograph by Sara Ann Harris)

The Spanish Louisiana settlers who relocated to Lower St. Bernard Parish called themselves Isleños. They lived off of the land and each person had a job. At a cultural revitalization event in 2000, Isleños posed as (bottom row from left to right) a game hunter, home cook, seamstress, guardian of the conveyance of public property, embroiderer, young girl, and coastal-bird catcher; (top row) duck hunter, fisherman, religious voice, and shrimper. The men wore the white uniforms of the Louisiana militia who fought the British during the American Revolution. (Courtesy Donna Mumfrey Martin, photographer unknown)

Cocoanut Island Dance Hall Bar (left) and a replica of Cocoanut Island Dance Hall (right). The dance halls served as Isleño trade centers during the Modern Age of Fur. When controversy between outside buyers and Isleños ensued over land ownership and the cost of pelts, conflict erupted at the halls. (Courtesy Donna Mumfrey Martin, photograph by Sara Ann Harris)

*Isleño decima singing at the Lower St. Bernard Parish dance halls grew out
of an Old World Spanish lyric-bard tradition.* (Courtesy *La Parranda de
Teror*, photograph by Sara Ann Harris)

Father and daughter Canary Islanders worked with local Isleños to prepare traditional Spanish dishes at the 2010 heritage fiesta. Potato frittata was their specialty. (Courtesy Donna Mumfrey Martin, photograph by Sara Ann Harris)

At heritage fiestas and community events, Dot Benge and Bertin Esteves employed dramatic dialogue to convey the story of the Canary Islanders' settlement in Louisiana. (Courtesy Dorothy Molero Benge, photograph by Sara Ann Harris)

Chapter 6

Folk Singing at the Dance Halls, 1900-65

By some accounts, a common language is the foundation of a community identity. The St. Bernard Parish Spanish dialect borrowed from several influences and was sustained at least through the Dance Hall Era. The Saturday-night gatherings cultivated the language: at the dance halls everyone spoke Spanish, told jokes in Spanish, and sang in Spanish. In a 1940s study of the St. Bernard Parish Spanish dialect, Raymond MacCurdy wrote that gatherings "in which jokes are swapped, stories told, and favorite songs lustily sung by one or more of the local bards . . . contributed in large measure to the preservation of a vigorous Spanish folk-culture."

Influences on the dialect streamed back to the Spanish takeover of the Canary Islands in the fifteenth century. Spanish nationals, primarily Andalusians (residents of the southern region of Spain on the shores of both the Atlantic and the Mediterranean), migrated to the islands. Many Portuguese also settled there; intermarried with Guanches, the Canary Island natives; and lived an agricultural life. There were several dialects spoken in Spain itself. Castilian Spanish was defined originally as the language of the medieval lyric poet knights who perpetuated a tradition of composing and performing song. The Andalusian, Portuguese, and Castilian dialects were all significant in the formation of Canary Island Spanish and, by extension, were basic to the Spanish dialect of St. Bernard Parish.

French planters worked lands that were later a part of St. Bernard Parish. When the Spanish Canary Islanders settled in the same region, they borrowed words from their French neighbors, particularly the names of items they were unfamiliar with, for example, words for Louisiana flora, fauna, and topography. Likewise, when a wave of Santo Domingan sugar planters settled in St. Bernard (1794), the Spanish Louisianans adopted some Caribbean Spanish terms. Over time there were other Latin American influences, as families relocated to St. Bernard from Cuba, Puerto Rico, and, to some extent, Mexico and Venezuela. Some Spanish Louisiana men contributed to the purity of the language when they traveled to Cuba, Mexico, and even Spain in search of Spanish-speaking women to marry and bring back to St. Bernard Parish. And in the twentieth century, a variety of Spanish nationals relocated to St. Bernard Parish. MacCurdy concluded, "The foundation of the Louisiana dialect in all of its aspects— lexicographical, phonological and morphological—is Spanish."

To negotiate their early life in the outside world, meaning the rest of southeast Louisiana, the Isleños learned to speak French and later English. Historian Alcee Fortier visited the Isleños in 1891 and wrote: "They all speak Spanish, but a few [also] speak the Creole patois [a local French and African dialect] and the younger ones speak English." During the Dance Hall Era, many more Isleños began speaking English, but the Spanish dialect of St. Bernard Parish remained the primary language of the community.

Particularly after their settlement of Lower St. Bernard and at least through the Dance Hall Era, the Isleños sustained a Spanish singing tradition that was a blend of Old World songs (including those from the Castilian lyric poetry tradition) and original a cappella compositions. They referred to this body of work as *decimas,* a term that loosely referred to a Spanish ten-stanza form. Performances by the Isleño *decimeros* (balladeers or troubadours) were the high point of the Saturday-evening gatherings. The singers found receptive audiences, especially at the early Delacroix dance halls. And as a form of preservation of the Spanish St. Bernard language, decima singing was a defining cultural tradition for the Isleños. Consequently, it attracted an impressive cadre of scholars who documented the musical heritage before it slipped away altogether.

I met Lloyd "Wimpy" Serigne at his home in central St. Bernard Parish. Wimpy's gruff voice belied his warmth and willingness to share memories about decima singing. He explained that during the Dance Hall Era, groups of men composed songs that poked fun at one another's character flaws. He started the story by providing a context. Shrimpers and fishermen began their work day well before dawn. They returned home to a late lunch prepared by their wives and then took naps. In late afternoon, the men gathered at the dance halls to visit, which invariably turned to teasing one another about missteps of the day. Then, one fisherman stood and sang his version of a jibe. He may have poked at a buddy for getting lost in the maze of bayous. A second singer then adlibbed a second stanza—embellishments were expected. Another guy followed, often employing a clever twist at the expense of someone else as a conclusion to the impromptu performance. There was a mood of jocularity among the men, and they competed to see who could dash off the funniest verse. They sang and carried on until they turned in for the evening.

"It's a story. That's all it [the decima] is," said Allen "Boogie" Perez. "It's poking fun in a friendly kind of way. It was nothing more than that. Not sarcasm . . . no. Just poking fun at someone for doing what they were doing."

On Saturday evening, after dinner, the atmosphere at the dance hall was electric. Everyone gathered at the edge of the dance floor and waited to hear this week's new decimas. The decimeros stepped out, their presence creating its own kind of limelight. As they each sang a stanza, it became clear who the target was. They did not need to use names. There were giggles and muffled laughs. Finally, the audience must have responded with an outburst of laughter at, say, the tale of someone burning spaghetti shrimp in a cast-iron pan or being kicked in the backside by a mule. The listeners were not shaming anyone; they were laughing at the fact that no one was exempt from life's little indignities. This brand of humor was an Isleño adaptation to life's twists or unexpected slaps.

The audience responded with guffaws, sideways glances, and finally rousing applause. These were people who lived side by side, blessed and burned by the same turns of fate. Their stomachs were full on a meal that was wholesome and delicious beyond what outsiders would have imagined. And they were being treated to a comedy act that only they could appreciate for its nuance. On the next Saturday, other singers excitedly awaited their moment. The audience tingled with expectation before the roast. Sometimes last week's roastees sang about their roasters. The hilarity went on week after week.

Pooka Perez added a variation on the story of how decimas were composed. He said that when something went awry, villagers sought out a particularly talented decimero and whispered the ridiculous scenario to him or her. For example, while unloading his catch at the seafood dock, a fisherman fell out of his boat. Well, in a culture in which your boat was your most important possession, how anyone could fall out of it makes a great joke. This story was fodder for the decimero's next composition and performance.

"The decimas were whatever had happened in the community that they were trying to hide," Pooka explained. "Well, naturally, the decimero would make a song out of it. And at the dance, they'd sing the son of a gun. Nobody knew exactly what was coming up."

Decimero Joseph Campo was known for his performance of *"La Pesca del Camarón"* ("Shrimping"). It was a tongue-in-cheek story about "Boy" Molero, a braggadocios shrimper. Boy was competitive—always claiming to outdo everyone else, whether it was with the best crew, the best catch, or the best boat. The song ribbed him about this bravado. On Saturday night, the audience must have held its breath in anticipation when Joseph stepped up to sing. A few lines from the song follow.

"La Pesca del Camarón"

A las cuatro la mañana, la compaña Boy presente;
el otro día a las seį, no habia caba barca gente.
Cuando Boy salió calando a esa mancha camarón,
'tuvo un mę y siete dią pálcontrá'l otro calón.
Cuando Boy siende las lusę y en el sentro del mar,
se queda todo alumbrá o como Caye'l Canal.
Boy mandó haser una barca, con una buena largura:
¡Cuando la prova 'šté aquí, que la popa en Chepitula!

"Shrimping"

It was four in the morning, all Boy's crew standing by;
at six the next day, they still weren't all on board.
When Boy went out fishing for that school of shrimp,
it took him a month and seven days to bring together his nets.
When Boy turns on the lights out in the middle of the sea,
everything lights up, as bright as Canal Street.
Boy had a boat built. and it was pretty long:
when the bow is here in Delacroix, the stern will be in Chepitula!

Note the references to New Orleans: Canal Street and Chepitula (Tchoupitoulas Street). Both are approximately thirty-five miles from Delacroix. The listener could easily hear the singer's taunting. The song teased Boy about his exaggerated opinion of his crew, boat, and shrimping expedition.

The Isleño repertoire also included songs that howled, like

wolves in the dark, or songs that bemoaned mishaps. These decimas were poetic commentaries on living and working in an unpredictable and dangerous world. The decimeros chronicled the daily vagaries of their lives. Paul Perez was a respected decimero and no doubt a regular performer at the dance halls. Allen "Boogie" Perez was Paul's son and learned to sing decimas from his father. I first met Boogie in front of a home he himself had built after Hurricane Betsy (1965). He was compact, with strong forearms, and seemingly had nothing to hide. We walked up a twenty-foot staircase and into his home. He was unhurried and ready with a quip. Yet his humor was understated and he hardly ever cracked a smile. After visiting with Boogie many times, I thought of him as not particularly needing to impress anyone. He was content living in Delacroix and said he would never leave.

His father had composed *"El Mosco y el Agua Alta"* ("Mosquitoes and High Water"). It was a much-loved commentary on a day in the life of a fur trapper. For the trapper, a season of mosquitoes and flooding was the worst possible scenario. Fierce mosquitoes meant there had been a mild winter, not cold enough to clear out the insects. A mild winter meant the animals' furs were thin, not what trappers needed to get a good price at the trade center.

Furthermore, flooding from heavy rainfall and river overflow would have forced animals to high ground, where trappers couldn't catch them. All in all, mosquitoes and high water meant a complete loss of income for the three-month trapping season— easily the most lucrative time of the year for the Isleños.

When I asked, Boogie agreed to sing the decima. He stood up from his overstuffed chair, took a moment, and then began in a deep melancholy voice. It sounded like the Negro spiritual "Nobody Knows the Trouble I've Seen" but without the utter dejection. Of course, he sang in Spanish and the lines rhymed. A couple of stanzas follow.

"*El Mosco y el Agua Alta*"

Esto si que son trabajo,
esto si que son fatigo,
que pasa un pobre trampero pa mantener la familia.

Ha'lcontrá'o el trampero está el mosco y el agua alta
y para cumpletá de la banca le mandan cartą.
Cuando yo yegué a casa, asi me dijo Sesilia:
"Padre, aquí tiene una carta que le mandan de la Villa."

"Mosquitoes and High Water"

This sure is hard work,
these sure are hard times,
that a poor trapper must go through,
just to feed his family.

The poor trapper finds out
there's mosquitoes and high water
and, to top it all off,
they're writing him from the bank.
When he got back home, Cecilia said to him:
"Father, here's a letter
that came from New Orleans."

"What's wrong? Why're you crying?" he asked.
"Father, they're asking you to pay off your full debt."

All the children gathered 'round
and we took each other's hands.
"Father, what're we going to do
when next summer comes around?"

Even though the trapping season had failed, the bank was pressuring the trapper to pay off his loan (to buy the land). His children were distressed. While the opening of the song bemoaned the trapper family's losses, in the remaining verses, the father consoled his children. He said they could reach out to family for assistance. If not, they would recover in shrimp season. If that failed, they could count on crabbing or fishing or duck hunting. This song documented a father teaching his family community reciprocity and adaptation to the misfortunes of their coastal life—a tenet of the Isleño character.

The Isleño singing tradition included comments on the complexities of wetland life and selections from an Old World Spanish music heritage. Seemingly, since their Louisiana colonization, Isleños had composed original works as well as passed on a body of Old World songs from generation to generation. True to the definition of folklore, the singing tradition was exclusively oral. The Isleños did not write down their compositions or read works from earlier generations.

Over time, Spanish emigrants from Galicia, Catalonia, Santander, and Andalusia contributed to the Isleño folk-singing tradition. Cuban and Santo Domingan singers also relocated to St. Bernard and influenced the musical repertoire. In addition, a few of the Isleño songs evidenced a Mexican influence. The community recognized individual balladeers for their singing talent, original compositions, and variations on Old World songs.

In the twentieth century, original Isleño compositions as well as songs from the Spanish tradition conformed loosely to five genres: (1) the song that poked fun at human foibles, such as "Shrimping"; (2) the poetic commentary on day-to-day life, such as "Mosquitoes and High Water"; (3) the ballad or telling of a romantic misadventure; (4) a local take on a national event or historical happening; (5) the oblique *corrido*, a song that drew on the audience's common knowledge. By definition, the corrido insinuated a story rather than used specific details to tell it.

Paul (Boogie's father) and Seraphin (Pooka's father) were brothers who grew up in Delacroix and sang a repertoire of Old World Spanish songs. Boogie said his father practiced while playing records on the family Victrola. Boogie remembered him singing *"Paloma"* ("Messenger Pigeon"), a ballad about a romance gone wrong. The protagonist, a young man, sent a love letter by pigeon to a woman for whom he yearned. The pigeon returned with a message, which he followed with an invitation for her to come visit him.

"Well, the pigeon came back with something like a Dear John letter telling him that she no longer cared for him," Boogie said. Still, he was going to pursue her—but the pigeon dropped dead on the ice. The bird was exhausted. This was, of course, interpreted as a bad omen for the romance. Samuel Armistead, a scholar of the Spanish ballad, explained that this folk literary form—the romantic-sexual relationship gone sour—was sung as far back as medieval times. Variations on the theme included marital fidelity, infidelity, and aberrations of love such as rape, incest, jealous vengeance, and murder.

As a boy, Pooka took an interest in the Old World songs and learned them. So he was allowed into the bar, which was strictly off limits to children. He remembered someone hoisting him up to sit on the counter; when the singing began, Pooka joined the gang.

"I was lucky enough, I guess, to have a fairly good voice," he said. "I was only maybe ten years old, twelve at the most, and they allowed me to sing . . . 'cause I knew all the decimas. I made it my business to learn them. I would sing for [in place of] whoever wasn't there at the time."

Pooka told me this story at the "Tribute to Storytellers," an evening of performance art at a college in Chalmette. He was on the program as a guest singer. That night, Pooka sang one of the popular ballads about the misfortunes of love. The protagonist was a soldier who had been away at war. In *"La Vuelta del Marido"* ("The Husband's Return"), on his return the soldier disguised himself and flirted with his wife to test her fidelity. He told her that her husband was dead and proposed to her. But his wife remained true, and she rejected him. Ironically, the husband was left to live alone.

When Pooka stepped out onto the stage, I imagined that we were all in the dance hall after midnight and the evening was peaking. Pooka stood alone in front of the Chalmette audience; his demeanor was calm and unaffected. His large hands hung easily at his sides. He closed his eyes and seemed to sink into himself to

As a boy, Irvan "Pooka" Perez sang with a cadre of decimeros (balladeers) at Delacroix dance halls. In later life, he performed decimas (Isleño folksongs) for the pleasure and edification of interested audiences across the state and the country. (Courtesy Carol Ann Perez Nunez, photograph by Sara Ann Harris)

gather the song. His singing voice had a lovely yodeling quality. An excerpt of the song follows.

"La Vuelta del Marido"

(esposa)
"*Soy una mujer casada recientemente;*
nadie tendrá mi amor.
Mi marido me dejó
para buscar su libertad."

(esposo)
"*Según lo que me dices,*
tu esposo está muerto.
Señora, si estás dispuesto,
ambos podríamos casados;
si usted y yo queremos
y si es voluntad de Dios."

(esposa)
"*Me miro en el espejo:*
'*Qué bonita viuda I'll be!*'
He esperado seis años para él
y esperaré más de seis años."

(esposo)
"*Mi esposa lleva luto,*
aunque nadie me ha matado."

"The Husband's Return"

(wife)
"I'm a recently married woman;
no one will have my love.
My husband left me
to look for his freedom."

(husband)
"According to what you tell me,
your husband is dead.
Madam, if you are willing,
we could both be married;
if you and I want to
and if it's God's will."

(wife)
"I look at myself in the mirror:
'What a pretty widow I'll be!'
I've waited six years for him
and I'll wait six years more."

(husband)
"My wife is wearing mourning,
though no one has killed me."

"La Vuelta del Marido" was a popular romance sung in all countries where Spanish, Portuguese, Catalan, and Judeo-Spanish were spoken. The pain of sincere love undone at the hand of mistrust was poignant. The audience applauded loudly. In all likelihood, some of them had once enjoyed Pooka's performances at the dance halls in Delacroix.

"*Lilola*" ("That's Life") communicated the Isleño take on a national happening—the employment program of the Great Depression. The 1929 crash on Wall Street impacted coastal communities around the country but not as deeply as it did those in urban locales. Coastal peoples lived with occupational self-reliance and the tremendous support of social togetherness. Also, their formula for a good life did not factor in a wealth of cash.

When the Works Progress Administration (WPA) went to Lower St. Bernard and provided government jobs, people appreciated it. Yet, the Isleños had always operated their own family businesses and perceived themselves as independent from the government. In addition, they were amused by what was considered dangerous on WPA jobs. Generations of Isleños had lived through hurricanes and floods—larger-than-life threats. They did not view a thorn or a minor ax injury as particularly alarming. According to at least one interpretation, they saw the jobs as superfluous. "*Lilola*" openly makes light of doing extraneous highway work under less-than-trying circumstances. The tone is tongue in cheek.

Following are three stanzas selected from the song.

"*Lilola*"

O lilola! Y a mi poco se me da!
Y el trabajo del welfare
e un trabajo muy regoso;
el probesito de Titico
se clavo un pico espinoso!

O lilola! Eso si que y e verda.
Para yo pasar trabajo,
Me quedo quieto en mi casa.
El probesito de Pirilla
se corto un pie con el hacha.

O lilola! Eso si que y e verda!
Y Lulo de Tio Jasinto
me vino a pidi un sombrero,
porque va co un golpe sol
al medio de un solajero.

"That's Life"

That's life! I just don't much care!
The work you do on welfare
is too dangerous for me;
poor little Titico
got a thorn in his foot!

That's life! That sure is the truth.
To go through all that work,
I'd rather stay back home.
Poor old Pirilla
cut his foot with an ax.

That's life! That sure is the truth!
Lula, son of Uncle Jacinto,
came to borrow my hat;
he's gotten a sunstroke
from working in the sun.

This last stanza refers to the fact that everyone in Lower St. Bernard worked out in the sun and weather, virtually every day of the year. It was unheard of and just plain silly that anyone would not know to wear a hat. The implication was that something that ridiculous could only happen when working for the government.

Because it required interpretation for the outsider, *"Lilola"* can be viewed as an example of the oblique corrido. It was allusive rather than narrative; it called on local common knowledge rather than provided details. Outsiders were not as likely as residents of Lower St. Bernard to appreciate these songs. *"Lilola"* and similar songs played like inside jokes. The song was based on a perspective that only locals were familiar with and could come across as vacuous to outsiders. The Isleños learned to live in the moment, however forceful the wind or high the storm surge. They had mastered the art of accepting life on life's terms. Composing and singing decimas, then presenting them at the dance halls, was one manifestation of that artistry.

At the dance halls after the decima singing, people began to head home. Parents picked up their children where they were sleeping on cots. The owner and his family cleaned up the kitchen. Men in the bar finished their card games. Then, the Isleños stepped out onto the dirt road and walked toward their homes. Some headed for nearby villages. A couple of pals might have sung a decima as they strolled, one guy's arm draped over the other's shoulder. Teenagers might have sleepily stumbled along behind their parents. At home, most of the family climbed into bed and dropped off to sleep. The fathers and sons, however, often changed to their work clothes and went directly to their boats, moored on the bayou behind their homes, and set out to shrimp, crab, or fish depending on what was in season.

Isleños sang, not just at the dance halls, but at weddings and christenings and on holidays. At Christmas, they processed from door to door and sang Spanish folksongs and seasonal melodies. It was customary for the balladeers to sip from small cups of blackberry wine at each stop.

A few individual decimeros were remembered for their passion. Boogie said his father, Paul, sang all the time. "My dad left the house in the morning. He left singing. When he arrived in the evening, he was singing. Even out in the marsh, my aunt would listen to him. She would sit out on the front porch and listen to my daddy while he was singing—out at the camp.

"Many, many times I was with him on the boat. Everything was going wrong. I mean everything. And I said to myself—I wouldn't say it to him; no, I wouldn't dare—what has this old man got to sing about?"

Experiences like these prepared Boogie for Isleño life. Decima singing, like their other cultural traditions, buoyed the Isleños through a flood of misfortunes. "Today, I realize that maybe one of the greatest things that was ever done for us," Boogie concluded, "was they [the parents in the village] showed us what life was like. They showed us the hard times. They showed us the good times." They learned to sustain themselves by accepting the hard times and creating the good times.

Louise Bonomo Perez truly enjoyed the Isleño decima singing and dance-hall experience in Delacroix: "They were fun people. They like to get together and sing the decimas. A group of people, they would compose them, and they would sing 'em.

"And then when they had a dance on a Saturday night, they all gather . . . it was quite a few dance halls for that little bitty place. The people would dance and the ladies would make the duck gumbo and the chicken gumbo and they would serve that.

"Oh, they used to have a lot of fun. Now, they were fun people. They used to love to gather . . . that would be all night long. That would be 'til daylight in the morning."

Chapter 7

Spirits and Smugglers at the Dance Halls

Early Spanish colonists of south Louisiana enjoyed a custom of liberal consumption of alcoholic beverages, a pleasure cultivated in their homeland. Like Spanish Catholics of the Old World, Spanish Louisianans imbibed freely while visiting and relaxing with friends. Everyone in the family, young and old, drank wine daily with meals. And following solemn rituals commemorating feast days of patron saints, Holy Days of Obligation, and other religious holidays, they celebrated with music and dancing, feasting, folksinging, and drinking homemade spirits.

In the Old World, drinking spirits was not only a cultural tradition; it was a health measure. Water was not safe to drink nor was it particularly tasty. Even well water could be tainted. "Just to have a glass of water [in Europe], you were taking a pretty big chance because they didn't have a way of treating water," said Stephen Estopinal, Isleño and author of novels set in the Spanish colonial era. "And they didn't know about boiling water."

In Spain, drinking preferences included homemade spirits: both fermented and distilled. Estopinal explained that "distilleries were very important because that was another source of liquid that was purified." In Spanish Louisiana, the purity of drinking water was also questionable. Families enthusiastically carried on the custom of producing spirits at home and served them at meals, get-togethers, and the church common grounds.

Their cultivation of fruit in the fertile soil of St. Bernard Parish lent itself to the fermentation of wine. Fermentation, basically, was the use of an agent to convert complex compounds into

Shrimpers, fishermen, and trappers gathered at the dance hall after work to relax. They nurtured an Old World tradition of preparing and imbibing spirits. (Library of Congress, Prints & Photographs Division, FSA/OWI Collection, LC-USF34-057303-D)

simple substances. Louisiana Spaniards fermented blackberries, muscadines, strawberries, and other fruit to process wine. That is, they used a ferment or agent, such as yeast, to break down the fruit into alcohol and carbon dioxide. Families also served cherry bounce, a liqueur they produced from fermented cherries, along with a variety of beers using well-established fermentation techniques. They started beers with the extract of selected roots and a malt, then flavored the brew with hops, an aromatic oil from a particular dried flower.

To produce whiskey, the Spanish colonists of St. Bernard Parish built home stills. First, they heated a starter mix that had been passed down from earlier days. When it vaporized, an essence, as it was called, separated out. As the essence cooled, it condensed into a whiskey. Another Spanish Louisiana distillation technique started with a grain, such as corn or barley. The Spanish colonists also distilled "rye" from crushed ryegrass seeds.

Centuries earlier, Spain had claimed the Canary Islands primarily to plant sugarcane. Spain also developed sugar plantations in South America and the Caribbean. Rum was a byproduct of sugarcane processing, and Spain developed an international rum trade. Then, in colonial Louisiana, Hispanics and others operated sugar plantations. In St. Bernard Parish, planters produced a rum-like drink called *tafia* at the sugar mills and sold it over the counter to locals at the end of the workday.

In Lower St. Bernard, Hispanics also planted sugar and sustained their drinking heritage. Deep in the wilderness, they produced their own wines, liqueurs, beers, whiskeys, ryes, and also rum. Today's elders testified to the vitality of the Spanish Louisiana spirits tradition in the early twentieth century. They said there were home stills everywhere in the parish.

In Ycloskey, one of the Isleño villages in Lower St. Bernard, I had the opportunity to sit down with elder Edward "Doogie" Robin, Sr., at his kitchen table. Doogie was from a fur-trapping, shrimping, and oystering family. At eighty-six years old, he owned and operated an oyster dock, and his three sons worked in the seafood business. Doogie was a slender man, his skin deeply tanned. He was dressed in loose-fitting cotton clothes and his dark hair was combed straight back. He looked well kept and seemed well adapted to the marsh. He spoke in a deep voice.

Doogie grew up during the early dance-hall days. Outside of Isleño homes and trapping camps, men's drinking preferences were becoming Americanized. They gathered at the dance-hall bars most evenings. Bar service included bottled wine, beer, and whiskey purchased from New Orleans vendors. Doogie said he saw bartenders hand customers a whole bottle each of distilled whiskey plus the mixers. Then, for that night, the men mixed drinks according to their own tastes. But revelers also ordered

Men gathered for a friendly shrimp boil in Delacroix. Even during the twentieth century, Isleños carried on a Spanish tradition of brewing, distilling, and imbibing alcohol. (Courtesy Carol Ann Perez Nunez, photographer unknown)

from a stock of homemade spirits blended with age-old knowhow using local ingredients.

I looked around Doogie's kitchen and noticed bottles of wine, liqueur, and whiskey lined up on a counter. It was a sizeable collection. When Doogie realized I was interested, he stood up, opened the refrigerator, and took out a recycled brandy bottle. *Blackberry wine* was written on it in Marks-A-Lot.

"I got friends of mine still making wine. This buddy of mine, he's from up the line [not in St. Bernard Parish] and he makes the wine. They been doing it for quite some time. And it's all good. Real good. Want a taste?"

I hesitated. I was amazed that I had the chance to sample drinks that had actually been served at the dance-hall bars. Next, Doogie took out a large mason jar. The liquid was perfectly clear. He unscrewed the metal top, set a saucer on the kitchen table, and poured out a puddle of moonshine. Then, he spooned up a taste and handed the spoon to me. "That's important stuff there, honey," Doogie said. When I sampled it, my mouth and then my throat burned hot. When I was able to vocalize, I sputtered, "Wow!" He said, "This is 180 proof." To demonstrate, he struck a match and eased it close to the saucer. The moonshine lit up and a flame danced over it. "That's how I was introduced to the stuff," he said of the match test.

Next, he offered me what had been a particular favorite at the dance-hall bars, coffee and whiskey. The Isleños were known for drinking unusually strong coffee. I sipped it from a metal shot glass. "How does that taste?" he asked. Lingering in the back of my mouth, the coffee tasted at least as strong as the whiskey. After I swallowed, I asked what kind of coffee he used. "Luzianne Dark Roast and Chicory. The strongest there is!" he replied. "So you add the whiskey just to calm the coffee down," I quipped. We both cracked up. "That's it, honey."

Then he observed, "We lived the best life. If you went hungry or thirsty, it was your fault." Doogie's zest for life exemplified the distinctive Isleño spirit. And as an Isleño gathering place, the dance-hall bar no doubt reverberated with it.

Drinking alcoholic beverages in Isleño dance-hall bars and homes was challenged before World War I by the National Temperance Movement. It led to the Prohibition Act of 1920. The law stated that it was illegal to manufacture, transport, or sell intoxicating beverages for consumption in the United States. In St. Bernard Parish, that applied to dance-hall bars.

Objection to alcoholic beverages in the U.S. was voiced at least as early as the turn of the twentieth century, when the next great wave of immigrants crashed onto the shores of the country. They built homes and churches and settled towns. Historically, the lifestyles of these newcomers had also embraced a relaxed custom

Cocoanut Island Dance Hall Bar, built in 1919, is the only existing structure of its function. It was built in Toca as an adjunct of a dance hall and now graces the St. Bernard Village Isleño center. (Courtesy Donna Mumfrey Martin, photograph by Sara Ann Harris)

of drinking, both homemade and commercially processed spirits. They readily built saloons, where they socialized and drank. In some towns, the saloons were the center of political discussion, and their owners were political bosses.

These foreigners with unfamiliar drinking customs, political views, and religious affiliations were unappreciated by some native-born U.S. citizens. The most stringent resistance to nonnatives came from white Protestants living in the Midwest, and they were particularly contemptuous of the Catholic newcomers. At the center of the movement was the Anti-Saloon League, a coalition of Baptist and Methodist ministers.

The Prohibition Act never had the support of the full U.S.

citizenry. Many objected on the basis that almost all constitutional amendments had addressed protecting liberties of the people. Instead, this one placed a restriction on people's social behavior. The liquor law *did* allow certain exceptions, and out of disdain, Americans fully exploited these loopholes. For instance, the Catholic clergy was allowed to continue to produce wine for church services and sales to parishioners. Consequently, output of the Catholic wineries grew more varied, more sophisticated, and quite voluminous. When the law conceded the right of rabbis to sell wine to members of synagogues for religious rituals, the rolls of Jewish congregations escalated. Pharmacists were allowed to continue to fill prescriptions for whiskey for medicinal purposes, and their sales skyrocketed. Finally, the sale of denatured alcohol for industrial uses was not prohibited under the liquor law; it was then renatured, flavored, and sold as a beverage.

The recent American immigrants responded by ramping up home production of alcoholic beverages and smuggling spirits into the United States from Canada, Latin American, and the Caribbean. Immigrants and other citizens of New York, Florida, and Louisiana took matters into their own hands and developed prosperous bootlegging operations. In southeast Louisiana, residents of St. Bernard, Plaquemines, Jefferson, and Orleans parishes were heavily involved in the transport and sale of contraband. The flow of alcohol in hotels, restaurants, and bars, such as the dance-hall bars, was constant.

New Orleans historically was a port city with international ties. So, the distribution system from the port to the interior of the country was already well developed. With its strong French and Spanish Catholic heritage, the region wholly resisted the new liquor law. St. Bernard Parish was located on the Gulf of Mexico coast, and residents had both historical and familial ties to the Spanish Caribbean Islands. Furthermore, they shared a language with their compatriots in these places. As longstanding family-business operators, Isleños could be fiercely independent and even contemptuous of government interference. All of these factors boded well for a particularly energetic bootlegging trade in St. Bernard Parish. Federal agents were charged with enforcement of the ban. The efficacy of the southeast Louisiana coast as a bootlegging center did not escape them. They kept local residents, political leaders, and owners of bars and gambling houses on their radar.

Neither the Isleño appetite for nor access to homemade and commercial spirits was curbed by the new law. Dance-hall owners and bartenders had personal contacts with local suppliers, who worked as small-time liquor bootleggers and with the Louisiana ringleaders. And the runners (drivers who hauled contraband from the parish coast to New Orleans) gathered after work at the dance-hall bars, as always a place of male Isleño social regrouping. They were shrimpers and trappers, people who built their own boats and were expert navigators. They were not career criminals who had previously made their living in gambling, prostitution, and drug dealing. Rather, for most runners, this was an innocuous method of enhancing the family income. Living in a remote region and operating family businesses, they seized every new opportunity. In fact, their survival depended on it.

Doogie's father had been a bootlegger, so he witnessed the comings and goings of the business at his home. "They would come—I'm going according to my daddy, because my daddy was a bootlegger. They [St. Bernard whiskey runners] would meet the boat out in the Gulf—big boats that come from Cuba. Most of them come from Cuba. They'd meet them out there with small boats. And they would bring it [whiskey] in [to St. Bernard Parish]. . . .

"They haul whiskey from Colombia and Cuba and all that in them days. It was against the law, naturally. People went to jail on account of it. It was against the law for them to come in with it, but anyhow they did."

When Doogie explained how bootlegging worked in St. Bernard, he emphasized that it was operated by a ring ("clique"): the Latino seller, the Louisiana buyer, the Isleño runners, the "supercargo" (the Latino contact onboard the cargo boat), and the truck drivers at the pickup site in coastal Louisiana. There was a strict division of labor. In advance, the buyer closed the deal with the Latin American seller. The buyer set rules for the exchange to ensure he received the product—all of it. He provided the runners with details about the cargo ship and pickup. Runners also knew the identity of the supercargo and the drivers back at the marsh.

Then, under the cover of night, the runners meandered through some twenty miles of bayous out to the Gulf of Mexico, where they motored another fifteen miles out to a schooner, cargo steamer, or other oceangoing vessel. Breton and Chandeleur islands were common rendezvous sites. Onboard, only the supercargo was authorized to approve handoff of product to the runners. The supercargo had to guard against giving the contraband to "rogue runners." The runners loaded the cargo onto their boats, motored back to the parish, and delivered it to the drivers. In the parish, runners kept an eye out for federal agents posing as drivers and hijackers aiming to heist the booty.

Running spirits wasn't for everyone. Doogie explained what it took for a man to join a smuggling clique: "This was all on nerve." He tapped the vein in his wrist, a colloquial gesture meaning the runner had to have guts. "Well, in other words, you really had to have this." He pointed to his vein again and said decisively: "Nerve. It was a chance you taking. You taking a chance of going out there and getting them [the cargo] and then maybe going to jail. Or maybe not even coming in with it. You just had to have a lot of nerve." It seemed he was saying that, for the runners, it was a point of pride to take on such a challenge.

After runners had picked up the whiskey out at the cargo steamer, things got dicey on the water. United States Coast Guard cutters were staked out and ready to hunt the runners down. There were all-out chases at high speeds on moonless nights, without boat lights. The Coast Guard agents were just as adept as the Isleños at handling their boats. The fishermen ran hard and cut frequently as they tried to outmaneuver the law. The runners resorted to various ploys to slip through the lawman's noose.

Isleños were known to modify their boat designs for speed and also used two or three engines at once. They installed cabins with bulletproof windowpanes or protective metal plates. They built secret compartments below, then packed the liquor in tightly and covered it with just-caught shrimp or fish. Back inshore, after completing a job, some runners sank their boats temporarily to avoid seizure by the Coast Guard.

When the runner made landfall, agents of the U.S. Bureau of Internal Revenue and the Department of Justice were nearby, sniffing for a scent. The shoreline of St. Bernard Parish is irregular. Multiple inlets lead to bayous and bays that are interconnected. This worked in the smuggler's favor. The locations of inshore hiding places and rendezvous points with drivers were difficult for outsiders to anticipate. Smugglers sometimes concealed the cache, up to six hundred cases of spirits, in the forest for later pickup.

There were other furtive exchanges. A Louisiana buyer had his drivers wrap the bottles and hide them in packing cases meant for canned vegetables or fruit juices. Drivers also transported whiskey in water bottles and gasoline cans. There were boastful stories like the one where the drivers loaded expensive champagne into a coffin and slid it into a hearse for transport. In a procession behind the hearse, there were grieving relatives, large, fancy bouquets, and concealed guns, all moving slowly up the road to New Orleans.

A story about a 1923 murder at Violet Canal Bridge was published by both St. Bernard and New Orleans newspapers. A buyer and his brother loaded a truck with their contraband at the canal and were preparing to drive up to New Orleans. Two sheriffs who had been lying in wait for bootleggers ambushed the criminals. Then, someone shot and killed both lawmen. It was never clear which bootlegger was the shooter.

Later, the brothers claimed that when they saw the sheriffs, they thought they were hijackers trying to heist their booty. One brother took the fall and was imprisoned for the murders. However, a powerful contact in the bootlegging business had arranged a deal with the Louisiana governor, and after one year, the governor pardoned the killer.

The Armbrusters once got in a tangle with Delacroix Island heisters. Andrew Pierce Armbruster operated a cattle business at Creedmoor Plantation in St. Bernard. His daughters Valerie and Andrea grew up there. Valerie became a pharmacist and Andrea was a schoolteacher at Delacroix Island School. Valerie said that one evening, the family drove to the Saenger Theatre in New Orleans in her father's elegant Pierce-Arrow automobile. When they came out of the movie house, they found the car had been stolen. It was a heavy automobile with backseats that could be removed to accommodate cargo.

The next day at Delacroix Island School, Andrea overheard the principal's husband bragging about stealing the car. Clearly, it would have been useful for hauling contraband into the city. One thing led to another and the car was returned, voluntarily. Valerie did not recall what consequences befell the thief.

Many of the Louisiana buyers were successful businessmen and public officials in St. Bernard Parish. It was a known fact that the parish deputy sheriff and district attorney worked in cooperation with New Orleans police officers to move booty from the parish to the city—once while flashing riot guns at the feds.

Doogie and others confirmed this: "And when they [runners] get the spirits in here [to the marsh], they met some high officials [local public leaders running the heist]. That's where the big bucks were. I remember a bunch of little guys [drivers] coming down here in their cars and putting it in the trunk and bringing it up [to New Orleans]. Boy, they [local public leaders] made serious money. They got big bucks. You know, if you got away with it. A lot of them got away with it. Quite a few got caught."

Estopinal recounted stories about St. Bernard and Plaquemines parish public leaders who were in cahoots with state police officers. They dodged the ban on alcohol as well as the prohibitions on gambling and prostitution. "The Highlight Club in Arabi was where they [anyone, including public officials] did a lot of gambling and stuff," such as prostitution and bootlegging.

"They used to collect the money and bring it down to their 'bank'—big quotes around bank . . . ," he said. "They would take the winnings and put it in the deputy's car and drive it down to the 'bankers' in Plaquemines Parish. . . . So, they [the public leaders] weren't really worried about the [local] authorities too much. They were the authorities."

Estopinal told another story about the involvement of St. Bernard Parish law-enforcement agents in crime. "The state police every once in a while would try and raid places [gambling houses]. Before the raid would happen, they [police] would call the Highlight Club and say, 'The state police are going to come raid you in about two hours.' So they [club owners] would have to take all the slot machines and load them on a truck and drive them around until the raid was over."

Generally speaking, enforcement of the liquor law was as chaotic in Louisiana as it was in the rest of the country. Court records were mishandled. The meting out of penalties for offenses was haphazard. To exacerbate the process, authorities put confiscated whiskey up for sale. Federal agencies were shorthanded and underfunded. Documentation of bootlegging rings and their violations, arrests, and convictions was thin. The federal Bureau of Prohibition, the official record keeper, estimated that 10 percent of U.S. bootleggers were caught.

At the Isleño dance-hall bars, the dancers, drinkers, balladeers, fur trappers, shrimpers, fishermen, rum runners, gamblers, fur buyers, and ringleaders rubbed shoulders with one another. The wheeler-dealer fur buyers and the bigwig whiskey smugglers were the real gamblers, flush with cash. Isleños covered the pool table with a board large enough to close off the pockets, then got the game rolling. Outsiders sometimes backed Isleño gamblers in order to keep the game exciting. Dween Nunez said, "They had an old pool table there and we used to shoot craps. We used to play craps. A fellow by the name of 'Joe'—he used to come from New Orleans. He had $100 bills in his pockets. At the craps table, he used to back the other gamblers. All around the table!"

Dween chuckled. "I seen plenty money! It wasn't *mine*—but I seen plenty." Dween was old school, and like other Isleño elders, he didn't see real value in greenbacks.

Other Isleño elders recounted anecdotes of the gambling life at the dance-hall bars. There was mention of a fur trapper, for instance, who gambled away his next two "lots" (sacks of pelts— one month's income) by the end of the night. And there was a savvy Isleño businessman famous for gambling with silver dollars. He occasionally strolled out of the bar to the dancefloor and tossed coins that youngsters happily snatched up.

Isleño socializing at the bar could get rowdy. The combination of spirits and money changing hands erupted into disagreements. That, or tensions from earlier in the week surfaced. It just wasn't Saturday night unless someone got riled up and punched somebody else. It was almost a ritual. One Isleño woman said that Saturday-night fights at the dance-hall bars gave everyone a chance to air their differences from the week before. Then on Monday, they could go back to shrimping, trapping fur, or running whiskey with a clean slate.

The dance-hall bars were gathering places that nurtured the male Isleño identity. Even while being scrutinized by the federal agents,

Spanish-speakers enjoyed a healthy appreciation of libations. Bars were havens for Isleño independence, in this case expressed as a reaction to government interference with their drinking tradition. They were also incubators for camaraderie, though in dance-hall bars it was exclusively male.

Shady characters emerged and suspect exchanges played out at the dance-hall bars during Prohibition. Bootlegging in St. Bernard was profitable for everyone involved, but more for some than others. With the 1929 Crash on Wall Street and the onset of the Great Depression, Prohibition and the whiskey-smuggling business ended. Isleño fun at the dance-hall bars over a glass of blackberry wine or a cold bottle of beer persisted.

Chapter 8

Revitalization of Dance-Hall Traditions, 1976-Present

The "Isleño" moniker was coined by the Spanish Louisiana villagers of Lower St. Bernard Parish in colonial times. Early on, they intermarried with the French and Cajuns who lived nearby. Into the nineteenth century, as some Isleños grew weary of the unpredictability of nature and longed for a stable income, they moved to central and then upper St. Bernard and joined with other Louisiana Spanish, Italian, and Irish families. Consequently, by 1960 the term "Isleño" had come to signify the link to a respected Spanish bloodline but not necessarily to Spanish cultural traditions or a distinctive wilderness character.

By 1960, the population of Isleños in central St. Bernard Parish had built what might be called modern dance halls or clubs. Isleños who once frequented these clubs said they did not necessarily host family events or draw Spanish-speakers exclusively. Some clubs held dances on holidays, such as Mardi Gras and Christmas, and women otherwise did not attend. Teenagers were carded. Few clubs served Louisiana Spanish dinners. Often, the dancefloor was in the bar itself, and instead of dancing to live music, Isleños danced to popular tunes on the jukebox. None of these neighborhood places featured decima singing. Nonetheless, today's Isleños told great stories about the clubs, and it sounded as though both Isleño affability and rowdiness prevailed there. The clubs in central St. Bernard were located along the Mississippi River and Bayou Terre-aux-Boeufs.

Mississippi River
Violet: Camellia Club, Dale's, Sam Nunez's, and Celi Perez's

Caernarvon: Blue Goose, Green Onion, Tootie's, and Steve's Dream
  Bar

Bayou Terre-aux-Boeufs
St. Bernard Village: Charlie Plush's
Toca: Cocoanut Island
Contreras Village: Three Leaves

I asked Allen "Boogie" Perez how long the more traditional
dance-hall galas of Lower St. Bernard lasted. He replied, "It
just kept fading out, and fading out, fading out." Another elder
suggested that Hurricane Betsy physically destroyed the last hall
in 1965. However, since some halls were still standing after Betsy,

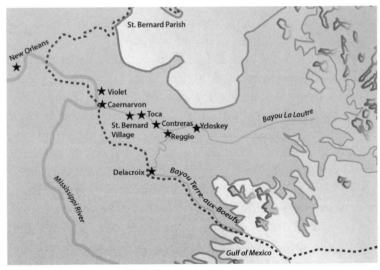

*The authentic dance halls (1900-) in Ycloskey (Vita Molero's, Mrs.
Martin's), Reggio (Teta's), and Delacroix (Tony Molero's, Vincente Fabre's,
Ernest Melerine's, Arthur Molero's) were sanctuaries of traditional Isleño
culture, located in Lower St. Bernard. Isleños opened other gathering places/
nightclubs upriver in central St. Bernard (1960-) that they also cherished.*

though in disrepair, perhaps the elder was using the physical and social displacement caused by the storm as a signifier of the close of the era.

By the end of the Dance Hall Era, the Isleño identity of Lower St. Bernard was morphing into that of a generic southeast Louisiana family. Instead of perceiving themselves as Louisiana Spaniards, many Isleños saw themselves primarily as fishing families struggling to make ends meet. The disruption to the coastal environment by oil and gas and navigation interests ultimately forced trappers to dismantle their family businesses. More and more families broke away from their isolated hamlets on Bayou Terre-aux-Boeufs and Bayou La Loutre to take jobs upriver in the manufacturing sector.

Isleño cultural traditions that had thrived at the dance halls abated. As public education became more widespread, everyone except the elders spoke English in Lower St. Bernard. There were families who continued to distill moonshine for home consumption, but men and even women were now more likely to buy alcoholic beverages from the nearby grocery store. Home cooks were still famous for Louisiana Spanish hot dishes, but there were fewer and fewer extended-family Sunday dinners. The Isleño passion for folkdancing to Hispanic string music was enjoyed only rarely and in family living rooms. And only when invited to, talented troubadours would sing decimas. Young residents said they didn't remember them singing at the dance halls at all.

Boogie talked about the state of the Isleño survival adaptations after the Dance Hall Era, i.e., their reliance on community reciprocity and their acceptance of life on life's terms. He said, "This generation that we have today is nothin' like we had. Nothin.' They have a different outlook on life. Which in some ways it kind of hits [upsets] me. And then I got to look back and say, well, I got to accept this. That's their way of life. It's not my way of life. They do things different. They think different." To hear him talk about this passing was saddening. But overall it remains easy to marvel, frankly, at a people whose Spanish Louisiana heritage thrived for nearly two centuries.

It was a fine day in 1976 when Frank Fernandez, St. Bernard Parish historian, emerged as an advocate of revitalizing Isleño customs. Fernandez and his partners did not aspire to rebuild dance halls or revive day-to-day Isleño cultural life. They wanted to produce presentations that featured Isleño customs that had peaked during the Dance Hall Era. The objective was to honor the Isleño people themselves and educate new audiences about a life that had been mostly hidden for 200 years in the shadows of southeast Louisiana.

A host of resourceful community members responded well to Frank's leadership. Isleños staged their first presentation in Lower St. Bernard, then moved their planning and production upriver to the St. Bernard Village area. In time, they formed two Isleño clubs, and each established a center for performances, events, and exhibits. These Isleño centers did not function as Saturday-night dance halls. They did not resuscitate the weekly joys and twists of fate that had played out there. Instead, the centers shone a light on Isleño customs that had had their final flowering at the dance halls. Over the years, organizers produced occasional events and then graduated to presenting an annual Isleño Fiesta. They broadened their coverage to include the Spanish Louisiana traditions of colonial times. To research those customs, Isleños visited the Canary Islands, brushed up on their Spanish, paired their dinners with Spanish wines, and danced and sang at feast-day festivals. Some Isleños forged friendships with Canary Islanders and they vacationed together—on both sides of the Atlantic. Around this time, Spanish Canary Islanders were staging their own cultural renewal. Isleños and Canary Islanders collaborated on their productions. In 1982, the Isleños invited a Canary Island dance club to perform in St. Bernard.

The National Park Service shouldered a leadership role. Parish political leaders and the Canary Island government provided financial support. As part of what can be referred to as the Isleño Revitalization, the community was also graced by the attentions of university historians, linguists, and anthropologists—from Louisiana, the United States, the Canary Islands, and Spain. They authored books, wrote dissertations, produced CDs of decimas, and video-recorded interviews of Isleños.

The air was crisp on opening day of the 2010 Isleño Fiesta, and silky white clouds splayed across a blue sky. I inched my way through the crowd toward the Cocoanut Island Dance Hall Bar, pausing to shoot pictures of a clever storyteller and then a grey-haired fiesta organizer shaking her finger at the sheriff and fussing about a mishap in the parking lot. At one point, I overheard Isleños speaking with visiting Canary Islanders in the same tongue. I felt as if we had been transported back to the islands in colonial times. Clearly, these peoples were of one and the same origin. That Isleños and Spanish Canary Islanders conversed easily in 2010 was a living testament to the durability of the Spanish language in Louisiana.

Before Hurricane Katrina in 2005, this Isleño center was an impressive assembly of lovingly restored homes of Isleño farmers, sugar planters, and fishermen. The cultural centerpiece of the landscape was the Cocoanut Island Dance Hall Bar, originally attached to a dance hall in Toca. The bar was the only surviving structure of its historic function in the parish. Katrina destroyed much of the center; some buildings could not be salvaged. The Isleños, led by St. Bernard Parish historian William de Marigny Hyland, had the structures rebuilt. A replica of Cocoanut Island Dance Hall was built, to the general specifications of the original building, and installed next to a repaired Cocoanut Island Bar.

At the fiesta, I strolled across the grounds toward the bar, then walked inside. I imagined fur trappers, shrimpers, decima singers, and whiskey smugglers drinking and gaming at the small wooden tables. Often, these men had been so preoccupied that they left their wives and girlfriends to dance with each other on the dancefloor. They had lifted their glasses in this very bar, toasting a win at the craps table. During Prohibition, libations flowed particularly freely and outsiders, anxious to capitalize on the booming Isleño fur and whiskey trades, had edged their way in and sat at the gambling tables on Saturday nights.

Fiesta planners showcased the Isleño fondness for spirits by serving Spanish wines. In the Middle Ages, with the rise of Catholicism in Spain, viticulture was greatly expanded. Spanish wines remain important today as both everyday table wines and high-quality wines. Fiesta-goers chose from offerings from the most famous winemaking regions: sherry from Jerez, tempranillo-based wines from Rioja, sparkling wines from Penedes, and garnacha (grenache) from Priorat. There was a holiday atmosphere at the bar as visitors sipped wine, sampled cheeses, and enjoyed tapas.

At the Food Pavilion, Isleños were engaged in large-scale food prep similar to the preparation for the midnight feasts at the dance halls. On the table, a grand variety of Louisiana and Spanish ingredients and eats were in various stages of preparation. Cinda Melerine was toiling over a kettle of caldo. When asked, she gladly identified the other dishes being prepared: chicken croquettes (crunchy fried morsels), paella (a rice and seafood favorite), shrimp and grits (a recently introduced, stick-to-your-ribs Southern dish), white beans (an early Isleño standard), empanadas (Hispanic ground-beef pies), and plantains (introduced to Louisiana by Spanish Caribbeans). A congenial man from Gran Canaria Island and his dark-eyed daughter smiled and agreed to be photographed as they worked. The man whipped a few dozen eggs deftly; then the young woman folded in chopped onions and cheese, sliced tomatoes, and chunks of peeled potatoes. They sprinkled in seasonings, poured the mixture into a large oblong baking pan, covered it, and slid it into the oven. After it was nearly cooked through, the woman withdrew the pan, uncovered it, and then returned the bubbling frittata to the oven to brown.

Nearby, a family of Isleño oyster farmers served a Louisiana delicacy: fresh, glistening, raw oysters on the half-shell, presented on a bed of sparkling chunks of ice. Louisiana seafood had been integrated into the Isleño culinary tradition as soon as the colonists settled in Lower St. Bernard. In south Louisiana at an oyster bar, if a guest hesitates, the oyster shucker dares him or her to consume the most plump mollusk on display. I hesitated. The shucker challenged. And I swallowed the bivalve whole. There was no other option.

The Isleño Revitalization generated a great deal of exposure in and out of Louisiana for Isleño customs. Isleños also exhibited trade arts such as boat building and wood-duck sculpture at their events. In addition to their own Fiesta, Isleños were regulars at the New Orleans Jazz and Heritage Festival and at state and national folk heritage festivals. They were recorded on video by the National Park Service for their oral history project. And *National Geographic* interviewed them for an article on Isleño history.

The Isleños were recognized for their passion for dancing from the moment they stepped onto Louisiana soil. At the dance halls, that passion expressed itself as unstoppable waltzing and jitterbugging to American styles of music. For their Revitalization, the Isleños decided to highlight the native folk dances that they had inherited from the Spanish Canary Islands.

Barbara Robin researched the music heritage of the Canary Islands in preparation for the formation of a local folkdancing club. A seamstress in the Canary Islands was contracted to custom-make authentic rural attire. And a dance instructor funded by a Canary Island grant traveled to St. Bernard and taught for a month.

Isleños also hired Donna Gagliano Gifford, a local dance instructor and choreographer. Donna was from one of the larger Italian families in St. Bernard Parish. She married Raoul Gifford, a Puerto Rican whose family moved to St. Bernard when he was a boy and blended seamlessly with the Isleño community.

Isleños attended dance lessons at Donna's Dance Studio weekly. The dance steps could be intricate. Some people were born dancers and others needed a little practice. "How do you expect us to do this?" a few of the novices asked. To keep it light, Donna made up funny names for unfamiliar steps.

"We had so much fun," she said. "I was teaching both the male and female parts." Once she was walking a man through *his* part and he began to lead. Donna stopped and said decisively, "I am the man. I *am* the man." Everyone laughed.

The Isleño group learned one dance from each of the seven islands and performed around the state at civic auditoriums and city parks. They also performed at Northwestern State University Folk Festival, the French Quarter Festival, and the Isleño Fiesta, where visiting Canary Island dancers observed. Donna said, "The look on their. . . you could see the pride in their faces that their heritage was being learned . . . that they were taking the time to learn the heritage dances."

Barbara Robin said her favorite performances were at the French Quarter Festival. She remembered once when the weather was lovely, the dancers' gaiety was contagious, and the crowd was responsive. Later, they were all proud when the Louisiana Department of Education published a history text for St. Bernard Parish schools and featured photographs of the group dancing in the Quarter.

Donna Mumfrey Martin applied her considerable talents to executing multiple presentations on Isleño trades and customs, including folkdancing. The most publicized Isleño dance performance was at the exposition of the Royal Collection from the Museo del Prado and Patrimonio Nacional, which was held at the Mississippi Arts Pavilion in Jackson and billed as including the largest array of Spanish royal treasures ever exhibited in North

Pino Hernandez Suarez of Gran Canaria Island (left) introduced locals to the joy of Spanish folkdancing at the 2010 Isleño Fiesta in St. Bernard Village. (Courtesy *Los Cabuqueros de Arucas*, photograph by Sara Ann Harris)

America. The Isleño dance club performed throughout the day at the cultural arts pavilion. In all, the club made appearances like this one for seven years.

Like other Isleño customs, decima singing was lapsing into obscurity as the dance-hall days faded. At about this time, linguists and anthropologists began working with the decimeros, men and women alike, including Josephine Acosta, Martin Alfonso, Joseph Campo, Paulina Diaz, Adam Hernandez, Julia Melerine, Laurencio Morales, Allen and Paul Perez, Irvan and Seraphin Perez, Malvina Perez, Nicolas Perez, and John Robin. These scholars recognized a community's language as key to preserving its identity. Some analyzed the linguistics of the Isleño decimas. Others concluded that the origin of the decima rested in an Old World minstrel lyric tradition. Linguist Raymond MacCurdy described Seraphin and Laurencio as "troubadours worthy of the tradition."

The Spanish Canary Islanders' passion for dancing drew onlookers out onto the fiesta dancefloor. (Courtesy Donna Mumfrey Martin, photograph by Sara Ann Harris)

There was a great demand for performances of the decima. Like other bearers of tradition, decimeros took part in the New Orleans Jazz and Heritage Festival and state and national folk heritage festivals. The Louisiana Folklife Center at Northwestern State recorded decimeros singing and distributed the CDs. A New York film company produced a documentary about Isleño fur trapping and featured the decima "Mosquitoes and High Water."

At their engagements, decimeros personally experienced the authenticity of the decima's link to the Spanish Canary Island culture. The Canary Island government invited Pooka Perez and Louise O'Toole to visit. University professors recorded their songs, examined the linguistics, and arranged for them to sing at local venues. One afternoon, Pooka sang a Spanish folk song he had learned from his father called *"La Huerfanita a la Orilla de un Palmar,"* or "The Orphan Girl at the Edge of a Palm Grove." A selection follows.

"La Huerfanita a la Orilla de un Palmar"

Y a l'orilla de un palmar,
yo visto uno joven beya,
con su labio de coral,
sus ojitos dos estreyas.
Al pasar, le pregunte
de quien vivia con eya.
Y me respondio, yorando:
"Solo vivo en el palmar.
Soy huerfanita,
no tengo padre ni madre,
ni un amguito,
que me quiera consolar.
Solita paso la vida,

a la orilla del palmar,
y solita voy y vengo,
como la sola del mar."

"The Orphan Girl at the Edge of a Palm Grove"

At the edge of a palm grove,
I saw a beautiful girl.
Her lips were of coral;
her eyes were two stars.
Passing by, I asked
who lived with her.
And she answered me, weeping:
"I only live in this grove.
I'm a poor little orphan.
I've neither father nor mother,
nor even a friend,
who might wish to comfort me.
I spend my life alone,
at the edge of this grove.
Alone I come and go,
like the waves of the sea."

After the performance, an elderly woman from the audience approached Pooka and a window to his past blew open. The woman exclaimed that she remembered her mother singing *"La Huerfanita"* when she was a child. It was a profound personal moment for Pooka and for the woman, one that revealed a living connection between the Isleño and the Canary Island music heritage. It was immediate evidence of the endurance of the Spanish Canary Island folksinging tradition in St. Bernard Parish.

Furthermore, researchers established that the song originated in eighteenth-century Spain and was sung in many regions of the Hispanic world.

Wimpy and Doris Nunez also had such an experience. One afternoon, I stopped by their home to ask if the exchange between Isleños and Canary Islanders had exposed any particularly obvious evidence of cultural continuity. Wimpy responded in his sonorous voice and Doris chimed in with almost-forgotten details that made the story work.

They had attended a performance by a Canary Island singing and dancing troupe at Nunez College in Chalmette. In the theater, the stage was set as an agricultural site in the late 1770s. It was a hat tip to *La Descamisada*, a custom that Canary Island corn farmers once practiced: as harvest season approached, farmers asked family and friends to help shuck and prep the corn for market. In the barn, as everyone sat on the floor and shucked, they sang to one another. Afterward, the landowner served a meal for the pleasure of all of the helpers.

The Canary Island performers onstage mimed planting and harvesting and then sat to shuck the corn. One person began to sing about someone who faltered in the field, impromptu and in jest. In response, someone sang a complementary verse; others laughed and carried on in this style. Wimpy spoke Spanish, so he understood the verses. But as he listened, he realized he was also familiar with the form. It was the spontaneous bantering of an Isleño decima.

A man might tease a woman about her cake falling, and a woman might quip that the man's machete was dull. The singers invited Wimpy onstage to participate in the lighthearted joking. He felt right at home. The custom of good-natured, impromptu, a cappella banter and the round-robin form were clear predecessors of the decima singing that so entertained the Isleños at the dance halls. The hair on Wimpy's arms stood up as he told me the story.

His experience was a testament to the persistence of a Canary Island singing form in Louisiana.

Canary Islanders of colonial days did not go out to professional theater openings, orchestra performances, or gallery exhibits. Like rural communities everywhere, they invented their own social entertainment. In the islands, Descamisada was a much-anticipated opportunity for young men and women to meet. Their bantering often softened to nudging and even flirting. One man may have caught a young woman's eye and sung about her lovely hair; another might have looked longingly at a woman nearby and sung about how flattering her dress was; and maybe another farmer's son would ask a young woman to take a walk in the moonlight. This variation on the banter form was also brought to life on the Nunez College stage.

Wimpy remembered one occasion when decima singing segued into romancing at a Delacroix dance hall. It was not a harvest party, nor did it lead to a first date. A betrothed Delacroix couple stood across the dancefloor from one another. The crowd hushed. The young man and woman sang in rounds expressing their amorous feelings; they pledged their hearts in the most sincere verses. Wimpy said there was no way to describe it. A link between this couple's romantic exchange and the Spanish troubadour tradition can only be suggested here.

There seemed to be no end to the possibilities for exposure of the decimas. Pooka Perez joined the dance club in their trip to the Mississippi Arts Pavilion in Jackson, which included a private audience with King Juan Carlos and Queen Sophia of Spain. He stood just ten feet from royalty and their entourage and performed in his melodious, lilting voice. Media from around the globe attended and publicized the events of the weekend.

In 1990, Pooka was invited to Carnegie Hall to perform as one of three Hispanic singers in an annual program called "Folk Masters: The Traditional Music in America Series." Nick Spitzer,

Isleño troubadour Irvan "Pooka" Perez (left) performed decimas for King Juan Carlos and Queen Sophia of Spain. Royalty were visiting the Mississippi Arts Pavilion in 2000 to view the Royal Collection from the Museo del Prado. (Courtesy Irvan Perez, photographer unknown)

now producer of "American Routes" broadcast by National Public Radio out of New Orleans, was artistic director and host for the evening. Pooka's wife, Louise, attended the ceremony. I asked her about watching Pooka perform. "I used to love it because I love the way he sings. He never was shy when it comes to singing. He used to love it, but he was not showing off."

The next year the National Endowment for the Arts invited Pooka to New York City. Charles Kuralt presented him with a National Heritage Fellowship for mastery of his art. Eleven other traditional artists were recognized at the annual awards program. That night Pooka sang "1777," his original historical piece about the

Canary Islanders' journey to Louisiana. I had had the opportunity to see him perform it at a local venue. He stood solemnly onstage, a solitary figure. He closed his eyes and readied himself. When he sang, his voice quivered with emotion.

In New York City, Charles Kuralt presented Irvan "Pooka" Perez with a National Heritage Fellowship for his mastery of the Spanish decimas. At the 1991 annual awards program, the National Endowment for the Arts recognized a dozen traditional artists in all. Perez had also been long respected for his artistry in sculpting Louisiana birds. When invited to sing decimas, he was often asked to display his most prized duck or songbird carving. (Photograph by Carol Ann Perez Nunez)

"Setecientos Setentaisiete (1777)"

Setecientos setentaisiete,
varias familias dejaron las Islas Canarias
para la costa de Cuba,
de la sur de la Luisiana.
Y en sur de la Luisiana
y entierra regalada,
se pusieron de jardinero
para mantenerse êstas familias.
Varias fueron de soldados;
peliaron por su libertá.
También salieron vitoriosos
y alcontra Inglatierra.

¡Viva Eŝpana y su bandera!
Que con tó mi corasón,
sé que simos Americanoŝ,
pero sangre d'eŝpanol.

Cuan' o'l tiempo se lę puso duro,
cuando no pudian má,
se fueron d'eŝta tierra,
y con otros es españolę,
se pusieron a la peŝca.
Entre'l pato y la rata,
entre'l agua y las pleŕia,
con el ayu' o de las mujerę,
se buscaron la via.
Con peną and tormento,
y la voluntary de Dio,
asina s'empuebló la costa
se la Parroquia San Bernardo.

¡Viva Eŝpana y su bandera!
Que con tó mi corasón,
sé que simos Americanoŝ,
pero sangre d'eŝpanol.

"Seventeen Seventy-Seven"

In seventeen seventy-seven,
some families left the Canary Islands
for the shores of Cuba
and southern Louisiana.
In southern Louisiana
and on the land that was given to them,
they became farmers
to maintain their families.
Some became soldiers;
they fought for their freedom.
They were also victorious
fighting against England.

Long live Spain and her flag!
For with all my heart,
I know we're Americans,
but our blood is Spanish.

When times got tough for them
and they couldn't hold out,
they left their land,
and with other Spaniards,
they became fishermen.
What with ducks and muskrats,
with the water and the marsh,

with the help of the women,
they earned their living.
With sorrow and trouble,
and by the will of God,
that's how they settled
the towns of St. Bernard.

Long live Spain and her flag!
For with all my heart,
I know we're Americans,
but our blood is Spanish.

The crowd was stirred by Pooka's heartfelt delivery of a song that recounted the story of a people who settled colonial Louisiana and who cherished a heritage both American and Spanish even into the twenty-first century.

The Isleño Revitalization successfully introduced thousands of people in Louisiana and well beyond to a community elevated in the first half of the twentieth-century at the dance halls of Lower St. Bernard Parish. This exposure, for the first time, cracked the edifice that historically had defined Louisiana culture as predominantly Gallic.

Index